THE
SOVIET POLICE SYSTEM

THE CONTEMPORARY SOVIET UNION SERIES:
INSTITUTIONS AND POLICIES

Each volume in the Contemporary Soviet Union Series examines in detail the facts about an important aspect of Soviet rule as it has affected the Soviet citizen in the 50 years since the Bolshevik Revolution of 1917.

Subjects include industry, culture, religion, agriculture, and so on. A careful examination of official Soviet material in each field provides essential basic reading for all students of Soviet affairs.

Robert Conquest is a former Research Fellow in Soviet affairs at the London School of Economics and Political Science and Senior Fellow of Columbia University's Russian Institute. His works include *Power and Policy in the U.S.S.R.*, *The Pasternak Affair: Courage of Genius*, *Common Sense About Russia*, *The Soviet Deportation of Nationalities*, and *Russia after Khrushchev*.

THE CONTEMPORARY SOVIET UNION SERIES:
INSTITUTIONS AND POLICIES
EDITED BY ROBERT CONQUEST

The
Soviet Police System

FREDERICK A. PRAEGER, *Publishers*
New York · Washington

BOOKS THAT MATTER

Published in the United States of America in 1968
by Frederick A. Praeger, Inc., Publishers
111 Fourth Avenue, New York, N.Y. 10003

Introduction © 1968 in London, England, by Robert
    Conquest

Library of Congress Catalog Card Number: 68-26180

Printed in Great Britain

Contents

Editor's Preface

This is a book on an extremely central and sensitive area of Soviet life and politics. As with the other books of this series, the text is essentially an array of primary source material, set in the appropriate historical and organisational framework. Here we may suitably sketch some of the more general (and human) perspective.

The *rationale* of the Soviet Police has always been that it is the 'Sword of the Revolution'. Its activities under the series of enemies of the people who headed it for the twenty years 1934–53 are not now receiving much praise (except in the case of the spies then recruited and utilised by it, like Philby). But its earlier, as well as its subsequent, conduct has been much idealised.

Right from the beginning it was treated as a very pure concentration of revolutionary probity, to the extent that its activities did not need to be restrained by legal or other considerations.

Its formation, on December 20, 1917, was more or less illegal. An informal 'decision' of the Council of People's Commissars was later represented as an official decree. It had no right under this supposititious decree to carry out executions. The first illegal execution took place in February, 1918. As one of its leaders wrote:

'Life had made it necessary to appropriate by revolutionary means the right to immediate execution. Comrade Dzerzhinsky had taken a step not foreseen by decree, not authorised by anyone. The Left Socialist Revolutionaries, heading the Commissariat of Justice, raised a cry, demanded that the question be brought up in the Council of People's Commissars. However, Vladimir Ilyich [Lenin] declined to include this question in the agenda of the *Sovnarkom*. He realised that Comrade Dzerzhinsky was right. One cannot go against life. In this way life itself legalised the right of the Cheka to immediate execution.'[*]

[*] M. Latsis in *Proletarskaya Revolyutsia*, No. 9 (56), 1926.

—this latter a singularly inappropriate phrase. An 'instruction' of September 17, 1918, finally empowered the Cheka openly to execute without reference to the Revolutionary Tribunals. And Lenin strongly attacked a 'narrow-minded intelligentsia' in the Party who were inclined to 'sob and fuss' about Cheka misdeeds.*

It has so far been the rule that the power and activity of the police have increased enormously during periods of crises in the Soviet Union, whether spontaneous or created by official policy (like the collectivisation terror). The first wave, starting in 1918 and culminating in the terror against the Kronstadt rebels, was followed by a period of comparative civic peace and stability, in which the Police's role, though never unimportant, was far less obtrusive. In 1930 came the collectivisation campaign which, by the beginning of 1933, left Police and Party victorious at the cost of the lives of millions of the peasantry. The Yezhov Terror in 1936–38 involved the use by Stalin of the NKVD as in effect his only weapon in destroying the old Party, disrupting all non-Stalinist loyalties, and packing the labour camps with millions of innocent citizens.

And here it will be appropriate to give a few Soviet descriptions of Stalinist police methods. Torture was explicitly justified:

'The Party Central Committee explains that application of methods of physical pressure in NKVD practice is permissible from 1937 on, in accordance with permission of the Party Central Committee. . . . It is known that all bourgeois intelligence services use methods of physical influence against the representatives of the socialist proletariat and that they use them in their most scandalous forms. The question arises as to why the socialist intelligence service should be more humanitarian against the mad agents of the bourgeoisie, against the deadly enemies of the working class and of the collective farm workers. The Party Central Committee considers that physical pressure should still be used obligatorily, as an exception applicable to known and obstinate enemies of the people, as a method both justifiable and appropriate.'†

An individual application of this doctrine may be seen in the

* *Pravda*, December 18, 1918.

† Circular coded telegram from the Central Committee, January 20, 1939 (quoted in Khrushchev's Confidential Report to the XX Party Congress).

following account of his experiences, by a Soviet general, published in the USSR:

'Even now my ears ring with the sound of Stolbunsky's evil voice hissing "You'll sign, you'll sign!" as I was carried out, weak and covered in blood. I withstood the torture during the second bout of interrogation, but when the third started, how I longed to be able to die!'*

A Soviet writer has remarked of the interrogators:

'They were all sadists, of course. And only a handful found the courage to commit suicide. Pace by pace, as they followed one routine directive after another they climbed down the steps from the human condition to that of beasts.'†

In this book we do not much elaborate on the rôle of the Police during the height of the Terror, giving rather that body's institutional history and present structure and mechanism. That is to say, we concentrate largely on the normal operation of the extra-legal organs. But all the same, their potential for excess, the threat of worse, is in many ways their most important element. This is so psychologically, in that Russians continually fear a reversion to Stalin's techniques. As one Soviet writer remarked, when congratulated by an American on the Khrushchevite 'Thaw', 'Yes, but what about yesterday—and tomorrow?'

In the new society Stalin created, police activity was no longer an emergency operation, but thoroughly institutionalised. After the death of Stalin, the surviving leadership showed some wish both to curb the Police in its capacity as a political entity dangerous to themselves, and to relax pressures in the hope that Soviet society would have achieved its own stability without needing too much in the way of coercion.

But towards the end of Khrushchev's tenure, and since, the Police have again tended to play an independent rôle. The KGB not only has its own professional interest in repression, but has also shown itself to be an important component of the 'reactionary' tendency in Soviet politics. On several occasions it has clearly undertaken independent actions not previously

* General A. V. Gorbatov, *Years off my Life*, English edition, London, 1964, p. 113.

† Evgenia Ginzburg, *Into the Whirlwind*, English edition, 1967, p. 52.

approved of by the leadership, in order to forward its own policies. The mustard-gassing of a West German engineer (see p. 95) in 1964 was a complete breach of discipline which would have been inconceivable under Stalin, and was instantly overruled by Khrushchev—then strong enough to fight back.

The intrusion of KGB into foreign policy which has followed has been even more remarkable. It would again have been impossible under Stalin for any demand to be made for the return or exchange of KGB agents in Western prisons. The Police are not in the position of power they held from March to June, 1953, when they were, to a large degree, flatly aligned against the Party apparatus. But they seem to be acting as a political interest in a way which can hardly be regarded with favour by any supporters of legality, let alone democracy.

One cannot avoid noting that the present leadership is composed of a generation the first steps of whose rise in the Party hierarchy were part of the internecine struggles of the Great Purge of the 'Thirties, in the period when those who failed to denounce their colleagues were specifically condemned.* Nor indeed has association with the Secret Police during its worst phases been any sort of handicap to political advancement. For example, Alexander Epishev, promoted to be a full member of the Central Committee after Khrushchev's fall and at present a prominent representative of the Party in military and literary affairs, was deputy head of the MGB during Stalin's last, Doctors' Plot, period.

It would probably be too much to expect of these cadres—or only exceptionally—any true revulsion in principle from terror or police rule. The hope has rather been that they might interpret their interests as requiring less terror. And to some degree this is clearly so. Nevertheless, they—or the majority of them—have already shown willingness to intervene by primitive police methods against even the most inchoate stirrings of a public attitude not wholly subservient to the Party apparatus.

For there has been no abandonment of the police machine's rôle as an institution for controlling the population in the interests of the leadership and of intervening wherever it is thought advisable, regardless of the law or of public opinion.

* See, e.g.: Circular Instruction of April, 1938, quoted in *Partiynoe Stroitelstvo v Sovetskoy Armii i Flote*, by *Yu. P. Petrov*, Moscow, 1964, p. 301.

Yet it is true that while using the Police to perpetrate various tyrannical, and indeed illegal, acts, the present rulers have evidently felt it in their interests not to abandon restraint and loose it on all dissent in the old Stalinist fashion. There are social and intellectual forces at work, a full-blown confrontation with which is not lightly to be undertaken. On the other hand the partial measures at present in train seem to result in nothing but further trouble. Meanwhile, we may in any case fruitfully study the nature and history of the police machine as it enters its second half-century.

Acknowledgements are due to H. S. Murray, and also to M. Friedman and A. Alexeyenko, for their invaluable collaboration.

ROBERT CONQUEST

I
Development of the
Soviet Police Apparatus

THE CHEKA

A special organ of police repression was created almost immediately after the 1917 October Revolution. This was the Cheka,
so called from the initials (VECHEKA) of the All-Russian
Extraordinary Commission. The Commission's full title was
All-Russian Extraordinary Commission for Combating Counter-revolution, Sabotage and Speculation, and it is stated to
have been set up by a 'decree' of the Council of People's Commissars of the RSFSR dated December 20, 1917.[1] It was, in
fact, the offspring of the military-revolutionary committee of
the Petrograd Soviet which had organised the October Revolution and of which Dzerzhinsky, head of the Cheka, had also
been a member. Under the terms of a law of November 2,
1918, it was to work in close contact with the People's Commissariat of Internal Affairs (NKVD) and with the People's
Commissariat of Justice, and was empowered to direct local
Chekas throughout the RSFSR.[2]

The Cheka was made officially subordinate to the supreme
governmental body, the Council of People's Commissars of the
RSFSR, by whom the chairman and members of its collegium
were appointed. The chairman of the Cheka also acted as a
member of the collegium of the NKVD. Both the central and
the local Chekas had their own 'armed detachments' separate
from the Militia (the Soviet equivalent of the normal police),
the latter being attached to the local Soviets of Workers' and
Peasants' Deputies and coming under the general supervision
of the NKVD.[3] The Militia, however, was to be at the disposal of
the local Chekas in so far as it was essential to the discharge
of their responsibilities.

Stalin in 1927 described the GPU and the Cheka as being
'more or less analogous to the Committee of Public Safety set

[13]

up during the Great French Revolution. It punishes primarily spies, plotters, terrorists, bandits, profiteers and counterfeiters. It is something in the nature of a military-political tribunal set up for the purpose of protecting the interests of the revolution from the counter-revolutionary bourgeois and their agents'.[4] During the Civil War the definition of counter-revolutionary activity or intent was a wide one. With the official announcement of a deliberate system of 'Red terror' on September 5, 1918, the central Cheka and the local Chekas were authorised to shoot 'class' enemies or isolate them in concentration camps.[5] The offences in respect of which the Cheka was permitted to exact 'direct retribution (up to shooting)' were specified in subsequent legislation. A decree of the All-Russian Central Executive Committee, dated June 20, 1919, listed among such offences the concealment of traitors and spies, concealment for counter-revolutionary purposes of lethal weapons, participation in arson, deliberate damage to railway and military installations, robbery and armed theft, and illegal plundering.[6]

The extra-judicial nature of the Cheka's powers was exemplified in a decree of October 21, 1919.[7] A Special Revolutionary Tribunal was created under the central Cheka, charged with waging a 'merciless struggle' against theft and speculation; the procedure laid down for it was 'in no way linked with the forms of jurisprudence'. In 1920 the Special Revolutionary Tribunal was abolished.[8] This did not, however, lead to any real decrease in the punitive powers of the Cheka, for under their existing regulations the ordinary Revolutionary Tribunals (before whom cases were now to be brought by the Cheka) had 'absolutely unlimited power to determine measures of repression'.[9] Moreover, in November, 1920, both the local Chekas and the Revolutionary Tribunals were invested with the powers of Military Revolutionary Tribunals, including 'the power of immediate execution of sentences up to shooting, but bringing each such sentence to the attention of the People's Commissariat of Justice and the All-Russian Extraordinary Commission'.[10]

During its existence from 1918 to 1922, therefore, the Cheka, like all its successors, combined both legal and administrative powers. As was stated in a 1951 Soviet legal textbook, 'the Extraordinary Commissions, while retaining their functions as organs for investigating cases for examination by the Revolutionary Tribunals, at the same time effected direct, extra-judicial suppression of counter-revolutionaries in the event of armed action on their part against the Soviet régime, in respect of banditry, etc.'.[11] Under the confused conditions of the Civil War, it is not known how many people fell victim to the Cheka. One reliable observer estimated it had shot 50,000.[12] It must have despatched many thousands more to prisons and concentration camps. As Bolshevik power established itself beyond the RSFSR, non-Russian Chekas were set up. One of the first of these was the All-Ukrainian Cheka, attached to the Ukrainian Department of Internal Affairs at the end of November, 1918.

The terror enforced by the Cheka was deliberately promoted by the Bolshevik leaders. On January 27, 1918, Lenin, addressing the Presidium of the Petrograd Soviet on the food shortage, declared:

'We can achieve nothing unless we use terror, and shoot speculators on the spot.'[13]

In June, 1918, Dzerzhinsky gave a Press interview in which he said:

'We stand for organised terror . . . Terror is an absolute necessity during times of revolution . . . We terrorise the enemies of the Soviet Government in order to stop crime at its inception . . . The Cheka is not a court. The Cheka is the defence of the Revolution as the Red Army is. And just as in the civil war the Red Army cannot stop to ask whether or not it may harm individuals . . . the Cheka is obliged to defend the Revolution and conquer the enemy, even if its sword does by chance sometimes fall upon the heads of the innocent.'[14]

THE GPU

With the end of the Civil War, the Bolshevik Government sought to achieve internal stability and external respectability. In December, 1921, the IXth Congress of Soviets called for a reorganisation of the Cheka and a strengthening of the bases of 'revolutionary legality'.[15] As Lenin had written in 1918: 'According as the basic task of the régime becomes not military suppression but direction, the typical form of suppression and coercion will become not shooting on the spot but the court.'[16] A decree of February 6, 1922, abolished the Cheka and set up the GPU (or in its full designation, the State Political Administration).[17]

Unlike the Cheka, the GPU was supposed to function under the direction of the NKVD as one of its subordinate departments. This meant that for the first time, both the Militia and the organ dealing with counter-revolutionary offences worked in single harness. At the same time, crimes against the régime which had been dealt with by the Cheka on its own authority were to be transferred to the courts.

The general codification of laws and the regularisation of court procedure which began effectively in 1922 were not accompanied by any apparent limitations on the administrative powers the GPU inherited from the Cheka. Contemporary legislation neither confirms nor denies the continuance of the plenary power to administer death sentences. The GPU did have the power of administrative banishment and exile for periods of up to three years, on its own authority, under decrees of August 10, 1922[18] and January 3, 1923.[19] The GPU also had wide powers of search and arrest and was required to conduct the investigation in cases of a political nature.

THE OGPU

When the RSFSR and the other Soviet Socialist Republics were reconstituted as the USSR, the first USSR Constitution, adopted in January, 1924, provided for an All-Union centralised body to direct the work of the local authorities of the GPU in the constituent republics.[20] This body was called the OGPU, its full title being the Unified State Political Administration. The OGPU had, in fact, already been set up by a law of November 15, 1923.[21] Unlike its predecessor, the GPU, the OGPU was not a part of the NKVD. Indeed after December, 1930, when the RSFSR NKVD and other Republican NKVDs were abolished, the OGPU had the monopoly of police functions in the USSR until 1934.[22] One consequence of this was that the Militia, which at least up to 1922[23] had been subordinate to the NKVD, was placed under the OGPU in 1932.[24] The OGPU had been authorised at the time of its creation to create a body of special troops and to organise border guards.

The continuity of the Cheka-GPU-OGPU was underlined by the fact that Dzerzhinsky, who had headed the Cheka from the start and the NKVD from 1920 and continued to serve as Commissar for Internal Affairs while the GPU was part of the NKVD, became chairman of the collegium of the OGPU. At the same time the OGPU did more than take over the function of preventing counter-revolution. During its 11 years' official

[16]

existence there began the piecemeal construction of the system of police controls over the daily lives of Soviet citizens. These controls had been largely unsystematised during the Civil War and the years of summary justice meted out by the Cheka, but they were now to become still more stringent and far more numerous.

The OGPU took over the considerable censorship of printed matter, plays and films acquired by the GPU in 1922 and 1923.[25] The first *Corrective Labour Codex* was drawn up in 1924;[26] the system of forced labour camps (though not that of colonies) which had existed in one form or another from September, 1918, was centralised under the OGPU, and official camp regulations were drawn up in 1930.[27] The administration of extensive frontier areas by the OGPU Border Guards was systematised in 1927.[28] The Soviet internal passport was introduced in 1932[29] simultaneously with the subordination of the Militia to the OGPU.[30] The networks of unpaid police ancillaries in villages and towns, known as 'rural executives'[31] and 'brigades for assisting the militia',[32] were given legal status.

The official imposition of these police-administered systems of control was not accompanied by any reduction in the existing police powers of summary jurisdiction. The law conferring powers of banishment and exile on the GPU was not repealed, and under a law of April 7, 1930, the OGPU was specifically authorised to send people to corrective labour camps.[33] As regards the power to impose the death sentence, a decree of March 14, 1933, stated that the 1923 law under which the OGPU had been established should be interpreted as giving it the power to 'take all measures of repression respecting the crimes of sabotage, arson, bombing, the destruction of machine installations in State enterprises and similar kinds of wrecking'.[34] Two days before the date of publication of this decree the OGPU announced that it had sentenced 36 people to be shot.[35]

The OGPU is inextricably associated with the earliest 'show trials' and with the mass repressions and deportations that followed the collectivisation drive launched in 1929. The numbers of those arrested, banished or sent to forced labour between 1929 and 1933 as a result of forcible collectivisation alone must be estimated in millions.

By a decree of July 10, 1934, the OGPU was absorbed into the People's Commissariat of Internal Affairs (NKVD) now recreated on an 'All-Union' basis.[36] The USSR NKVD remained in control of all Soviet police forces for seven years up to February, 1941.[37]

In the NKVD the Soviet police forces reached their full development and the USSR finally evolved the widespread system of police controls which is substantially that of today. The structure, functions and powers of the NKVD underwent no fundamental change in subsequent years; they were only reapportioned periodically among the two Commissariats (after 1941) and (after 1946) the two Ministries concerned—those for Internal Affairs and for State Security.

On the 'All-Union' basis all NKVD organs in the constituent republics came under direct control of the central NKVD, and the chain of command by-passed local and republican governmental authorities. In the RSFSR there was no separate People's Commissariat but a plenipotentiary of the NKVD of the USSR.

It was stated in the deree of July 10, 1934, that the new NKVD would be responsible for safeguarding revolutionary order and State security; safeguarding public (Socialist) property; recording acts of civil status (births, deaths, marriages and divorces); and safeguarding frontiers. The range of its responsibilities is more clearly evident from the list of its subordinate departments given in the decree. These were:

    the Chief Administration of State Security (GUGB);
    the Chief Administration of the Worker-Peasant Militia (GUM);
    the Chief Administration of the Border and Internal Guard (GUPVO);
    the Chief Administration of the Fire Guard (GUPO);
    the Chief Administration of Corrective Labour Camps and Labour Colonisation (GULAG);
    the Department of Acts of Civil Status (ZAGS); and
    the Administrative-Economic Administration.

Other subordinate bodies later added to the NKVD were:

    the Forest Guard (transferred from the People's Commissariat of Agriculture to the NKVD by a decree of September 21, 1934.[38] Two years later, control of this

[18]

body passed to an administration under the Council of
People's Commissars of the USSR);[39]

Chief Administration of State Surveying and Cartography
(set up under the NKVD by a decree of June 15, 1935.[40]
Three years later control of this body passed to the
Council of People's Commissars of the USSR);[41]

Central Administration of Highways and Asphalt Roads
and Auto Transport (transferred to the NKVD by a
decree of October 28, 1935.[42] This was renamed the
Chief Administration of Highways of the NKVD by a
decree of March 3, 1936);[43]

Colonisation Department (created in place of the All-
Union Colonisation Committee);[44]

Chief Administration of Weights and Measures (handed
over to the NKVD by a decree of June 26, 1936.[45] Two
years later this was in turn abolished and replaced by a
Committee for Affairs of Measures and Estimating
Appliances under the Council of People's Commissars
of the USSR by a decree of September 5, 1938);[46]

Chief Archival Administration (set up under the NKVD in
1940);[47]

Chief Administration of Hydrotechnical Construction (set
up under the NKVD by a decree of September 11,
1940);[48]

Chief Administration of Local Anti-Aircraft Defence (set
up under the NKVD by a decree of July 2, 1941);[49]

Chief Administration of Railway Construction (referred to
in 1941 State Plan of Development of the National
Economy of USSR).[50]

The Central Administration of Convoy Troops of the USSR
was disbanded and its forces incorporated in the NKVD's
Chief Administration of the Border and Internal Guard by a
decree of September 17, 1934.[51] The functions of the subordinate administrations mentioned are discussed later.

Between 1934, when the NKVD assumed centralised direction of the entire police apparatus, and 1941, when the NKGB
(People's Commissariat of State Security) first emerged as an
independent body, the Soviet police not only increased their
already wide field of competence but also contrived to enhance
their reputation at home and abroad as an instrument of ruth-
less repression.

The Stalin Constitution of 1936, hailed then and afterwards as a triumph of 'democracy, justice and freedom', did not terminate or even restrain the arbitrary powers and practices of the Soviet police. The political trials of the early 'thirties flared up anew late in the decade. The mass arrests and purges in Party and governmental circles touched off by Kirov's murder in Leningrad in December, 1934, were intensified after 1936. In 1937 the Armed Forces were the chief victims, and in 1938 the NKVD itself was purged.

Under the 1934 law founding the 'All-Union' NKVD, a body called the 'Special Board' (*Osoboe Soveshchanie*) had been set up. On November 5, 1934, this Special Board was empowered to impose banishment and exile, or imprisonment in a corrective labour camp for periods of up to five years.[52] The NKVD could choose between handing over cases it had investigated to the courts and handing them over to the Special Board, subject only in the latter case to the right of the USSR Prosecutor to address a protest to the then Presidium of the Central Executive Committee. There is, of course, no reason to believe that the powers of the Soviet police in practice were only those provided for in law. Not only do the experiences of those who escaped to tell of the purges of the 'thirties suggest otherwise but in 1938 many NKVD interrogators were themselves made scapegoats for having extorted false confessions and exceeded their powers.

The war years saw certain changes in the official designations of the NKVD. It had been divided on February 3, 1941, into two People's Commissariats, that for Internal Affairs (NKVD) and that for State Security (NKGB),[53] but after war had broken out with Germany a decree of July 20 re-established the NKVD in sole control.[54] Again in April, 1943, the NKVD and the NKGB were re-established as separate Commissariats[55] and this position lasted until 1946. Then, in consequence of the redesignation of all the People's Commissariats as Ministries, the NKVD and NKGB became the MVD (Ministry of Internal Affairs) and MGB (Ministry of State Security) respectively.[56]

For all these titular changes, however, the Soviet police pursued substantially the same tasks during the war as they had before it. They assumed a major part in the organisation of civil defence and in enforcing the rationing system. They supervised the far stricter wartime system of labour direction. They performed their regular counter-intelligence functions among the civilian population and in the Armed Forces. At the same time the police forces, and more particularly the border, internal and operational troops, were engaged on two major tasks of a less routine nature. Firstly, they acted as 'blocking detachments' posted in the immediate rear of forward army units. Their duties were not only to apprehend enemy paratroopers and spies but also to detain and execute summary justice on Red Army men fleeing from forward positions. Secondly, they organised the mass deportations of Soviet nationalities. The deportations began with the Volga Germans in August, 1941,[57] and ended with the Tatars in June, 1944.[58]

THE MVD AND THE MGB

After the war the NKVD and the NKGB (from 1946 the MVD and the MGB) continued their mass repressions. In Germany, counter-measures were taken through the police 'special departments' in the armed forces known as 'Death to Spies' (*Smersh*).[59] This organisation was particularly active in repatriation screening camps where its victims were Soviet ex-POWs and Soviet *Ostarbeiter*, as well as Soviet Army personnel who had fought in the Vlasov army. *Smersh* was also directed against the German population. Within the Soviet Union there were mass deportations from the Baltic States up to 1949, and other deportations from peripheral areas such as the western Ukraine, Moldavia, and the Caucasus. The peacetime controls were again enforced in all their complexity and the gradual severance of contacts with the outside world was accompanied by growing emphasis on internal vigilance and by suspicion of all individuals who had come into contact with the Western Allies during the war.

The continuity of the Soviet police apparatus has not been paralleled by similar continuity in leadership. Dzerzhinsky, and after him Menzhinsky, ruled supreme from 1917 to 1934. Then came the troubled period of the late 'thirties when Yagoda and Yezhov fell in quick succession. In the post-war period Beriya, who had been People's Commissar for Internal Affairs from 1938 to 1946, co-ordinated the work of both the MGB and the MVD. The MGB was headed by Merkulov for a short time, from mid-1946 by Abakumov, and subsequently by Ignatiev. The MVD was led by Kruglov.

From 1949 onwards the MGB enlarged its scope at the

expense of the MVD. In addition to the functions concerned with counter-intelligence and State security, originally allotted to the NKVD's Chief Administration of State Security (GUGB) and passed on to the NKGB, the MGB took over the Militia from the MVD. This probably occurred at the end of 1949, but concrete evidence dates from 1950.[60] The border troops were gradually transferred to the MGB during 1950.[61] In all probability the internal troops, who normally came under the same command as the border troops, were also handed over to the MGB, and it may well be that the same thing happened to the railway troops, who had close association with the Militia.

As a result of these transfers, the MGB for a time took over major responsibility for both repressive and 'policing' functions, the latter including the internal passport system and the registration of births, deaths and marriages; the MVD became predominantly an economic and technical agency. It continued to run the forced labour camps through GULAG; to supervise the construction of State highways through *Gushossdor*; to mine most of the USSR's gold and precious metals through its Far Eastern forced labour camps; to control the fire protection system of the entire country; to assist *Glavlit*, the official censorship body; to share in the organisation of civil defence; and to exercise responsibilities for hydro-electrical construction. It seems doubtful whether during the period 1950–52 the MVD had any major forces of police troops subordinate to it, with the possible exception of the convoy troops. Even these, though closely associated by nature of their work with the MVD-run GULAG, were formally, by virtue of an earlier law, a part of the Chief Administration of Border and Internal Troops, which evidently came under the MGB.[62]

It appears that the redivision of functions did not last even until Stalin's death. Possibly as early as January, 1953, the MVD had regained control of the frontier and internal troops, though the MGB at that stage was still apparently in charge of the Militia.[63] Immediately after Stalin's death on March 15, 1953, however, the MGB was absorbed into the MVD.[64] Thus for one year the MVD alone discharged the police, security, Intelligence, administrative, penal and economic functions that had last been vested in one body in 1941–43. At the same time Beriya took over personally as Minister of the MVD from Kruglov,[65] while the former Minister of the MGB, Ignatiev, was dismissed from all his appointments.[66] When Beriya was arrested in June, 1953,[67] Kruglov resumed his post as Minister of the MVD, and in December came Beriya's execution.[68]

During its year of sole control (March, 1953–March, 1954) the MVD lost several of its economic functions. Three important cases in point were the temporary transfer of forced labour institutions from GULAG to the Ministry of Justice, probably in the summer of 1953; the transfer of responsibility for the construction of State highways to a new ministry created for this purpose in September, 1953; the transfer of responsibility for hydro-electrical construction to the Ministry of Electric Power Stations and of Electric Industry probably in March, 1953; and the transference of *Dalstroi*, the largest of the MVD's economic enterprises in the Far East, to the Ministry of Metallurgy (subsequently the Ministry of Non-Ferrous Metallurgy) in the summer of 1953.

THE MOOP AND THE KGB

The major outcome of cutting down the MVD apparatus in the period after Beriya's execution was the re-emergence of a separate State Security organ in March, 1954, in the shape of a Committee of State Security attached to the Council of Ministers of the USSR, known from its initials as the KGB.[69] Serov, former First Deputy Minister of the MVD, was appointed to head it, Kruglov continuing in charge of the MVD until he, too, on the eve of the XX Party Congress, was replaced as MVD head by a Party Central Committee functionary, Dudorov.[70]

The KGB started off by taking over responsibility for espionage and counter-espionage, running Soviet and foreign agents abroad and maintaining a special counter-intelligence service within the Soviet Armed Forces. But during the next three years, by and large it retrieved its pre-1953 position at the expense of the MVD. In June, 1957, it became apparent that the KGB had resumed control of the Border Troops.[71]

The MVD, on the other hand, lost ground not only to the KGB but also to other official organs. The MVD Special Board was abolished in September, 1953, though this was not announced until January, 1956,[72] and its Military Tribunals were also done away with in the same month. The fact that it soon afterwards regained control of the corrective labour camps in early 1954 from the Ministry of Justice was but partial compensation, since from 1953 onwards the forced labour system had been considerably cut down in scope and jurisdiction by amnesties and other legislative and administrative measures. Moreover, the MVD was subjected to far-reaching personnel changes that started before Dudorov took office and continued afterwards; the upshot of these was a sharp increase in the number of senior MVD posts held by Party officials, a cross-posting to the MVD of MGB/KGB officials and, in some cases, of Army officers, while those who were edged out were largely the old MVD career men.

The post-1953 reorganisation of the Soviet police apparatus has to be viewed in a special context. In the summer of 1953, Beriya was arrested; trials and executions of police officials continued up to April, 1956; and early that year Khrushchev delivered his 'secret speech' to the XX Party Congress.

The accompanying revelations made between 1953 and 1956 not infrequently hit hard at the past record of the Soviet police apparatus—but the two morals officially drawn were that the police apparatus must not be put over the Party and Government (as Beriya had sought to do) nor was there to be harnessing of its coercive potential to the cult of the individual (as Stalin had done).[73]

Khrushchev told the XX Congress that 'proper control by the Party and Government over the activity of the organs of State Security has been established'.[74] The network of departments of administrative organs, which stretches downward through the Party pyramid, starting at the top with the Central Committee's Department of that name,[75] has been the main instrument for Party supervision of the police. Since the dismissal of Serov in December, 1958, the KGB has been headed by Party functionaries: first by Shelepin, until November, 1961, then by Semichastny, until May, 1967, and since then by Andropov. Along the line of the Soviets, supervisory commissions for corrective labour establishments were set up in 1957;[76] MVD and Militia organs at regional (*oblast* and *krai*) level were reorganised into combined Administrations of Internal Affairs (UMVD) and subordinated to the *oblast* and *krai* Soviet Executive Committees in the autumn of 1956.[77] So, too, Militia departments in towns and *raions* were made subordinate to the local *Ispolkom*. Thus a system of 'dual subordination' was set up for the MVD.[78]

In January, 1960, the MVD was decentralised by the abolition of the USSR Ministry in Moscow and the transfer of its functions to the Republican MVDs,[79] which in August, 1962, were redesignated Ministries for the Preservation of Public Order (MOOPs).[80] Like most Khrushchev reforms this was unscrambled by the post-Khrushchev régime, which declared that the decentralisation had caused 'many difficulties',[81] especially in the work of the Republican MOOPs. In July, 1966, the MOOPs were recentralised[82] by the establishment of a USSR MOOP under Shchelokov, a party official associated with Brezhnev (appointed in September, 1966).

In contrast to the MOOP, the KGB is exempt from the system of dual subordination, and it is specifically stated that 'the local organs of the KGB ... are not subordinate to the local organs of State power'.[83] Moreover the KGB administers its frontier troops on an All-Union basis, by-passing republican and other local governmental authorities.[84] Since the early 'sixties its major concerns on the home front appear to have been 'economic crimes' (this has involved an extension of KGB investigatory powers and of the death sentence), and 'ideological subversion' and other security problems posed by the increased flow of foreign tourists, students, diplomats and other visitors. Among its most-publicised recent exploits have been the bringing to trial of Penkovsky and Wynne[85] (the Soviet official and British businessman sentenced in May, 1963, for espionage); Gerald Brooke[86] (the British lecturer sentenced in July, 1965, for trying to disseminate anti-Soviet propaganda); and Sinyavsky and Daniel[87] (two Soviet writers sentenced in February, 1966, for publishing abroad under pseudonyms works hostile to the Soviet régime).

The post-1953 controls and checks imposed on the police apparatus mean that extra-judicial powers and procedures are no longer readily available to it: they do not mean that the apparatus has been finally curbed. The scope and nature of police activity over any given period are by and large dictated by current Party policy, which itself is always subject to tactical changes. Soviet practice has demonstrated, for example, that official disgraces and rehabilitations originate not from considerations of public welfare but from those of political interest. However tightly the police are bound to the Party wheel, whenever the Party leadership falls short of unanimity or Party interests conflict sharply with the public interest, the existence of a police apparatus of the Soviet type is an invitation to act otherwise than by persuasion.

In any event, apart from the question of the exercise of overt political repression, the system of widespread quasi-political controls which the police apparatus is called upon to administer continues in being, and the responsibilities it enjoys range over a still broad field.

The present strength of the forces at the disposal of the MOOP and the KGB cannot be accurately established since no figures have been published, even for the Militia.

An officer who served in the MGB up to 1953 gave the following estimate of the strength of the police forces, excluding the Militia:

Internal troops	150,000
Convoy troops	100–150,000
Railway troops	100,000
Operational troops	100,000
Border troops	300,000
Guard troops	150–200,000
Approximate total strength . .	1,000,000

These forces were believed to include a number of tank and artillery formations. It seems likely that this figure should now be reduced by somewhere about one-half. In addition to them account has to be taken of the Militia: its numerical strength is considerable.

To sum up, the present MOOP/KGB, like their predecessors, have considerable forces at their disposal; are invested with administrative powers which, though more narrowly defined and less arbitrary than they used to be, are still considerable; are charged not only with the maintenance of civil law and order but also with the safeguarding of 'political' law and order; and, above all, are responsible not to the people but to the Party apparatus as the embodiment of the State.

SOURCES

1. In fact there is no such decree in RSFSR Laws for 1917 or any subsequent year.

What appears to be an extract from a hastily written minute of a 'decision' by the Council of People's

Commissars, dated December 20, approving the organisation of the Cheka, was first reproduced in the memoirs of a prominent Chekist, Latsis (*Proletarskaya Revolyutsiya*, 9 (56), 1926, pp. 81–97), and later by Pokrovsky (*Pravda*, December 18, 1927). Pokrovsky admitted that this 'decision' was not a decree.

2. RSFSR Laws, 1918, 80: 842.

3. RSFSR Laws, 1918, 75: 813.

4. Stalin, *Works*, Vol. 10, p. 212.

5. RSFSR Laws, 1918, 65: 710; *see* also *Pravda*, September 6, 1918.

6. *RSFSR Laws*, 1919, 27: 301.

7. RSFSR Laws, 1919, 53:504.

8. RSFSR Laws, 1920, 22–3: 115.

9. *Ibid.*

10. RSFSR Laws, 1920, 89:454.

11. Karev (D. S.), *Sovetskoye Sudoustroistvo*, p. 78.

12. Chamberlin, Vol. 2, pp. 74–5.

13. Lenin, Vol. 26, p. 457.

14. Bunyan, p. 227, quoting *Svoboda Rossii*, June 9, 1918.

15. Karev (D. S.), *Sovetskoye Sudoustroistvo*, p. 78.

16. Lenin, *Sochineniya*, Vol. 27, p. 236.

17. RSFSR Laws, 1922, 16:160.

18. RSFSR Laws, 1922, 51:646.

19. RSFSR Laws, 1923, 8:108.

20. Constitution of the USSR, 1924, chap. 9, arts. 61 and 62.

21. RSFSR Laws, 1924, 12:105.

22. The RSFSR People's Commissariat of Internal Affairs was set up on December 26, 1917, and abolished on December 15, 1930; *B.S.E.*, 1st edn., Vol. 41, p. 201.

23. RSFSR Laws, 1922, 33:386.

24. USSR Laws, 1932, 84:518.

25. RSFSR Laws, 1922, 40:461; RSFSR Laws, 1923, 14:177.

26. RSFSR Laws, 1924, 86:870.

27. USSR Laws, 1930, 22:248.

28. USSR Laws, 1927, 62:624 and 625.

29. USSR Laws, 1932, 84:516 and 517.

30. USSR Laws, 1932, 84:518.

31. RSFSR Laws, 1924, 28:266.

32. RSFSR Laws, 1930, 25:324; RSFSR Laws, 1932, 38:173.

33. USSR Laws, 1930, 22:248.

34. USSR Laws, 1933, 19:108.

35. *Izvestiya*, March 12, 1933.

36. USSR Laws, 1934, 36:283.

37. Decree of the Presidium of the Supreme Soviet of the USSR, February 3, 1941; *Vedomosti Verkhovnogo Soveta SSSR*, 1941, No. 7.

38. USSR Laws, 1934, 49:385.

39. USSR Laws, 1936, 35:311.

40. USSR Laws, 1935, 49:416.

41. USSR Laws, 1938, 41:236.

42. USSR Laws, 1935, 56:452.

43. USSR Laws, 1936, 14:121.

44. USSR Laws, 1936, 37:322.

45. USSR Laws, 1936, 33: 304.

46. USSR Laws, 1938, 40:231.

47. USSR Laws, 1940, 3:96.

48. USSR Laws, 1940, 25:608.

49. USSR Laws, 1941, 16:314.

50. *Gosudarstvenny Plan . . . na 1941 god*, appendix No. 128, p. 483.

51. USSR Laws, 1934, 48:372.

52. USSR Laws, 1935, 11:84.

53. Decree of the Presidium of the Supreme Soviet of the USSR, February 3, 1941;

Vedomosti Verkhovnogo Soveta SSSR, 1941, No. 7.

54. Decree of the Presidium of the Supreme Soviet of the USSR, July 20, 1941; *Vedomosti Verkhovnogo Soveta SSSR*, 1941, No. 33.

55. Vlasov and Evtikhiev, p. 192.

56. Decree of the Presidium of the Supreme Soviet of the USSR, March 15, 1946; *Vedomosti Verkhovnogo Soveta SSSR*, 1946, No. 10.

57. Decree of the Presidium of the Supreme Soviet of the USSR, August 28, 1941; *Vedomosti Verkhovnogo Soveta SSSR*, 1941, No. 38.

58. Decree of the Presidium of the Supreme Soviet of the RSFSR, June 25, 1946; *Izvestiya*, June 26, 1946.

59. 'Smersh' is believed to have existed from 1942 to 1946 and to have been headed by Serov and Abakumov. *Slovar Sokrashchenii Russkogo Yazyka*, p. 391, defines it as having been 'the special department in the armed forces'.

60. e.g. a Decree of the Presidium of the Supreme Soviet of the USSR, dated November 1, 1950, published in *Vedomosti Verkhovnogo Soveta SSSR*, 1950, No. 36, establishing a new medal to be awarded to, among others, 'the organs of the Militia of the Ministry of State Security'.

61. Evidence of the transfer was the creation of a medal for MGB border troops by a Decree of the Supreme Soviet of the USSR, July 13, 1950; *Vedomosti Verkhov-nogo Soveta SSSR*, 1950, No. 20.

62. USSR Laws, 1934, 48:372.

63. Bomash refers (p. 80) to the 'frontier and internal guards of the MVD, USSR and persons in the officer corps of the MGB (including the Militia)'.

64. *BSE*, 2nd edn., Vol. 27, p. 532.

65. *Pravda*, March 16, 1953.

66. *Ibid.*, April 7, 1953.

67. *Ibid.*, July 10, 1953.

68. Shot on December 23, 1953; *Pravda*, December 24, 1953.

69. Decree of the Presidium of the USSR Supreme Soviet, March 13, 1954, first published in *Pravda*, April 28, 1954.

70. *Pravda*, February 1, 1956.

71. *Trybuna Ludu*, June 9, 1957.

72. *Sovetskoye Gosudarstvo i Pravo*, 1956, No. 1, p. 3.

73. *See*, e.g., Decree of the Central Committee of the CPSU of June 30, 1956, 'On Overcoming the Cult of Personality and its Consequences', *Pravda*, July 2, 1956.

74. *Pravda*, February 15, 1956.

75. Evidence of the inter-relationship between the police apparatus and the Party 'Administrative Organs' network is to be found, *inter alia*, in the composition of conferences and seminars in this field referred to in *Pravda*, August 4, 1955; *Sovetskaya Latviya*, March 3, 1957; *Zarya Vostoka*, April 16, 1958; and *Sovetskaya Yustitsiya*, 1958, No. 4, p. 78.

76. *Sovetskaya Yustitsiya*, 1958, No. 2, p. 54.

77. The All-Union law in question has not been published; its incorporation into the Republican Constitutions followed shortly after, e.g., in Tadzhikistan by a Decree of the Presidium of the Tadzhik Supreme Soviet dated December 18, 1956—*Kommunist Tadzhikistana*, March 16, 1957. *See* also M. V. Barsukov, *Sovetskoye Gosudarstvo i Pravo*, 1957, No. 2, pp. 36–7.
78. *Ibid.*
79. *Pravda*, January 14, 1960.
80. *Vedomosti Verkhovnogo Soveta RSFSR*, 1962, No. 35.
81. *Sovetskaya Rossiya*, November 10, 1966 (interview with Shchelokov).
82. *Pravda*, July 28, 1966.
83. *ESPZ*, p. 96; *Sorokin*, p. 245.
84. As evidenced by references to such bodies as Frontier Troops Commands of 'the South-Western Frontier' (*Moscow Radio* Home Service, August 17, 1958) and of the 'Southern Maritime Frontier' (*Moscow Radio* Home Service, May 28, 1958) and the 'Far Eastern Frontier District' (*Komsomolskaya Pravda*, April 11, 1958)—bodies which, by reason of the area they cover, cannot but come directly under the control of the central KGB apparatus.
85. *Pravda*, May 8–12, 1963.
86. *Pravda*, July 23–4, 1965.
87. *Pravda*, February 11–15, 1966.

II
Size, Organisation and
Personnel of the Soviet Police Forces

There are no official statistics on the Soviet police forces as a whole or on any of their branches; there are only occasional references by name to certain of the forces concerned and certain of the tasks they perform. Soviet laws were fairly explicit on these tasks up to the mid-1930s; afterwards the references became few and less explicit. Estimates by Soviet refugees are necessarily fragmentary and those by Western observers conjectural. Thus, in the sense that information about the police is withheld from the Soviet people as well as from foreigners, the entire Soviet police organisation, with the partial exception of the Militia, must be classified as 'secret'. Similarly all Soviet police forces are in the nature of things 'political', in the sense that they act as instruments of the Communist régime.

THE MILITIA

This body is at present organised under the Chief Administration of the Militia (GUM) of the USSR MOOP. In October, 1917, when the Militia was first created, it was placed under the local Soviets of Workers' and Peasants' Deputies.[1] A year later the Militia was also put under the overall direction of the NKVD of the RSFSR.[2] In April, 1919, it was militarised[3] and by 1920 five specialised types of Militia had developed:[4]

(a) Urban and district (*uyezd*) Militia;
(b) industrial Militia (factory, forest, mine, etc.);
(c) railway Militia;
(d) water (river and maritime) Militia;
(e) criminal investigation Militia.

These branches were all administered by the Chief Administration of Militia of the NKVD of the RSFSR and supported from the NKVD budget. A system of dual subordination was provided for in that the local Militia organs were responsible both to the corresponding Soviet Executive Committee and to their superior Militia administration. By 1931 the Militia in the USSR were organised in Chief Administrations under the Councils of People's Commissars of the Union Republics, with local Militia organs still in dual subordination.[5] The cost of the general Militia was met from local resources, and the industrial Militia from contracts with the organisations it guarded. In December, 1932, direction of the Militia was centralised in the OGPU's Chief Administration of the Worker and Peasant Militia[6] and then, in 1934, in the NKVD of the USSR.[7] In 1935 the State Automobile Inspectorate was transferred to the Militia for the inspection, regulation and registration of motor transport, garages and drivers.[8]

The Militia is at present subdivided into:[9]

(a) Territorial Militia;

(b) Transport (railway and water transport) Militia;

(c) Administrative (*Vedomstvennaya*) Militia—for guarding various official installations and buildings, the underground, the drainage system, etc.

The Militia's present functional subdivisions include:[10]

Department for Combating Theft of Socialist Property and Speculation (OBKHSS);

Department of Criminal Investigation;

Passport Service;

State Automobile Inspectorate;

Patrol Service (*Naruzhnaya Sluzhba*), which has the task of 'preserving public order in public places';

Department for Visas and the Registration of Foreigners (OVIR).

The main tasks of the Militia include:

(a) operation of the internal passport system;

(b) supervision of persons sentenced to exile and of certain categories of people after their release from places of detention;

(c) enforcement of laws with the right of arrest, entry and search;

(d) enforcement of regulations concerning firearms, printing appliances, poisons, radioactive substances, seals and stamps, photography, etc.;

(e) control of address and information bureaux;

(f) collaboration with house administrators and caretakers, people's squads, border troops, etc.;

(g) dealing with waifs and strays and juvenile delinquents, and maintaining certain institutions for them;

(h) maintenance of order in public places and during parades, demonstrations, etc.;

(i) traffic control and supervision;

(j) investigation and prevention of crime;

(k) tracing of lost persons and those evading military call-up;

(l) issuing of passports and visas to Soviet citizens travelling abroad;

(m) registration of foreigners other than those (e.g. diplomats) registered by the Ministry of Foreign Affairs;

(n) detection and exposure of persons leading an 'anti-social, parasitic mode of life'.[11]

Militiamen may be armed while on duty, and may use their weapons 'as an extreme measure', in circumstances such as armed resistance to arrest.[12]

The organisational structure of the Militia, its duties, powers and conditions of service, are laid down in statutes adopted by the USSR Council of Ministers on August 17, 1962. But these have apparently not been published. Since 1956 the Militia has returned to the system of dual subordination nominally in force in the period 1917–31. *Oblast/krai* Militia Administrations no longer exist as separate bodies but are incorporated in the *oblast/krai* Administrations for the Preservation of Public Order which are theoretically subordinate to the Executive Committee of the corresponding local Soviet, on the one hand, as well as to the next highest body of the Ministry for the Preservation of Public Order, on the other. The head of the *oblast/krai* administration for the preservation of public order is simultaneously head of the *oblast/krai* Militia. At the lowest level Militia organs are departments of the town or *raion* Executive Committee. Militia Administrations at republican level are included in the Republican MOOPs and are co-ordinated by the central GUM of the USSR MOOP.[13]

Various measures were taken in 1962 to build up the authority and prestige of the Militia. They included, in addition to new Statutes, the introduction of a Militia Day (November 10), oath-taking ceremonies, red banners, and better equipment.[14] Moreover, a law was passed 'on increased responsibility for attacks on the life, health and dignity of Militia officials and members of People's Squads', which provided for the death penalty in the most serious cases of such attacks.[15]

But the impact of these measures appears to have been negligible, for the post-Khrushchev régime has found it necessary to return to the problem of strengthening the Militia, and has alleged that under Khrushchev its rôle was 'underestimated', and its staff 'unjustifiably' reduced.[16] Since Khrushchev's fall there have been increases in pay and in staff, and a further attempt to improve equipment.[17] To strengthen Party control and indoctrination of the Militia, the post of 'deputy head for political-education work' has been established in local Militia organs.[18]

BORDER TROOPS

These are subordinate to the KGB as a Chief Administration of Border Troops.[19] In 1918, Border Chekas were set up by those Provincial (*Gubernii*) Chekas whose territory included frontier areas. In 1922 the GPU was called on to 'assure the political security of the frontiers of the USSR',[20] and in 1923 provision was made for the formation of a Border Guard by the OGPU.[21] A 'Chief Administration of the Border and Internal Guard' was set up under the NKVD in 1934.[22]

There are three forms of border troops: Land Border Troops, Maritime Border Troops, and Aviation Border Regiments. Of the last two little is known, though the 1941 State Plan provided for the supply of 12 seagoing cutters to the NKVD in that year alone,[23] and both formations continue to exist.[24]

Frontier districts are distinct from military districts, and do not necessarily coincide with them.

Among the tasks of the border troops are:[25]

(a) the repelling of armed incursions into Soviet territory, and the protection of the frontier population and State and private property;

(b) the prevention of illegal entry or exit and, with the Customs Authorities, of the smuggling of goods, literature and foreign currency;

(c) the regulation of movement within the frontier areas and of movement into them from elsewhere within the country, in collaboration with the Militia;

(d) the maintenance of frontier markings;

(e) the pursuit and detention of those infringing frontier regulations;

(f) the prevention of illegal fishing by assisting the Fisheries Inspectorate;

(g) the enforcing of rules for navigation in Soviet territorial waters.

They also played a prominent part in the wartime and post-war mass deportations.

INTERNAL TROOPS

These are subordinate to the MOOP,[26] presumably as a Chief Administration of Internal Troops. In 1918 the Cheka had 'basic armed detachments' at its disposal.[27] Among the actions in which they participated were the suppression of the Kronstadt rebellion of March, 1921, and the struggle against the first stages of the Antonov rising in Tambov. In 1923 a body of 'special troops' was created, directly subordinate to the Chairman of the OGPU.[28] In 1934 a Chief Administration of the Border and Internal Guard was set up under the NKVD.[29]

Internal troops are distributed in special districts that do not coincide with military or border districts. Little is known for certain of their tasks, and official mentions are confined to the fact of their existence. They occupy barracks or camps in most large towns. It appears that they also help to guard Government buildings and to provide official bodyguards. There is eyewitness testimony that internal forces assisted in the rounding-up operations that preceded the mass deportations of certain Soviet national minorities in 1943 and 1944.

CONVOY TROOPS

These came under the MVD,[30] and are now presumed to be subordinate to the MOOP. Under the GPU's powers of banishment laid down in 1922 and 1923, provision was made for escorting prisoners either beyond the confines of a given area or to a banishment area,[31] and under the 1920 law on the NKVD Militia provision was made for the creation of 'special reserves' to 'accompany' people under arrest.[32] Specific mention was made in 1924 of the convoy troops of the GPU,[33] but it was not until 1925 that a Central Administration of the Con-

[34]

voy Guard was set up, appointed by the Council of People's Commissars of the USSR in agreement with the NKVD of the Union Republics.[34] In 1930 this body was renamed the Central Administration of Convoy Troops.[35] Finally, in 1934, this administration was disbanded and the convoy troops were transferred to the Chief Administration of Border and Internal Guards of the NKVD.[36] Their present functions are the same as in 1923.

GUARD TROOPS

These also come under the MOOP.[37] The law on the Militia of 1920 listed an industrial Militia as one of the branches of the NKVD Militia forces.[38] Under the law of 1922 the Militia were given the further task of guarding buildings of All-Union and special importance (i.e., telegraphs, telephones, posts, etc.) and forced labour and concentration camps.[39] By 1925 the industrial Militia had become the 'administrative Militia'.[40] Under a 1931 law this was formed *ad hoc* on the basis of contracts concluded by heads of Militia administrations of Union Republics, *krais* and Autonomous Republics with individual State institutions and enterprises, who paid for its services.[41]

The guard troops are a composite force. In Soviet sources they are variously referred to as internal guards, departmental Militia, militarised guards, armed factory guards and corrective labour camp and colony guards.[42] In the case of industrial installations, such forces are normally attached to the nearest territorial Militia organisation. There is also a special night guard service over commercial premises, shops, store depots, etc., attached to the Militia but supplied to the outside organisations concerned on a contractual basis. The Ministry of Railways maintains its own 'militarised guards'.[43]

FIRE GUARDS

Fire Guards were controlled by the MVD under a separate Chief Administration with local units at Republic, *oblast* and town levels. They are now run by the MOOP, and contain militarised elements and parachute detachments of air guards for fighting forest fires. They are authorised to impose fines for infringements of fire precaution regulations and to conduct inquiries into such infringements and into fires.[44]

This list of Soviet police forces is not exhaustive. There are specialised units with a certain measure of autonomy, such as the Administration of the Kremlin Guard. During the war the police organised 'special communications troops', which 'ensured stable and secret communications between Party and Government leaders and the High Command, and Fronts and Armies, and cleverly prevented attempts by enemy agents to break the communications'.[45] 'Special communications' continue to exist, and the KGB may well have responsibility for them.[46] At one time the police appeared to be in charge of railway troops but these now seem to come under the Ministry of Defence.[47]

RECRUITMENT AND TERMS OF SERVICE

There is little up-to-date official information about recruitment to the police organs and the terms of service with them. Earlier Soviet legislation, however, gives some indication of the probable present position.

The 1931 law[48] on the Militia laid down that members must give a written undertaking to serve for not less than two years. It also named certain privileges they enjoy, such as reduced rents. The non-commissioned and officer staff of the Militia, from the rank of sergeant upwards, are recruited under the terms of a 1936 law,[49] from the internal and frontier guards and the Army; from those graduating from Militia schools; from the ranks of the Militia and other NKVD organs; and from persons 'despatched by the Party and Government' to work in the Militia. Party membership in the police forces is very high. In 1963 it was stated that 93 per cent of border troops' officers were Party members or candidates and that the majority of other ranks were in the Komsomol.[50]

The seniority of the State security organs over the other police organs was evident from the 1935 provisions[51] governing service in the Chief Administration of State Security (GUGB). These stated that 'all persons of the officer corps of the Chief Administration of State Security of the rank of Senior Lieutenant and higher are in a position of command with respect to all ranks of junior commanders and leading staff of the Border and Internal Guard of the USSR'. This is likely to continue to be the case. Several senior officials of the KGB (e.g. Zakharov, the first deputy chairman, Zyryanov, commander of the Border Troops) hold the rank of Colonel-General; while

Shchelokov, in charge of the USSR MOOP, is only a Lieu-
tenant-General.

It would seem that the frontier and internal troops depend
for their privates and NCOs on national service drafts. For
those assigned to the internal troops, the term of service is
three years for privates and two years for NCOs, and in the
frontier troops three years for privates and NCOs.[52] Officers,
on the other hand, serve as regulars for a period of normally
25 years.

Members of operational police forces appear to receive
more numerous allowances than their counterparts in the
armed forces. Those above the rank of sergeant in both the
State Security and the Militia forces could not, according to a
1936 law, be arrested without the special permission of the
supreme authority in their own organisations.[53] A further
feature of Soviet police service, which applies equally to the
armed forces, is that, with the exception of the MOOP fire
guards, there are no units indigenous to a given area. This
principle applies particularly to the Border Troops.

STATE EXPENDITURE ON THE POLICE FORCES

Since 1940 no separate figure for expenditure on the police
apparatus has been given either in the Budget estimates or in
the declared Budget expenditure. The main allocation to the
police forces in the Soviet Budget is known to be included
among the allocations to certain other Ministries and official
bodies, principally governmental and judicial ones, collectively
designated as 'expenditure on the maintenance of the organs of
State administration'. The total allocation under this heading
is not mentioned in Budget estimates or recorded in the Press,
but is read to the Supreme Soviet by the Minister of Finance
and is subsequently met with occasionally in textbooks on
finance. At the same time the figure publicly given in the
Budget estimates under the heading 'administration' is believed
to cover all the departments and services included in the vote
for the 'organs of State administration', other than the police
ministry or ministries.

On the basis of Soviet data it has been estimated that the
approximate share of the police in the Soviet Budget since
1934, when the NKVD first took over the central direction of
all police functions, is as follows:

		Budgetary Expenditure on the Police Apparatus (Thousand Million Roubles)	As Per Cent of Total Budget
1934	. .	1·1	2·0
1935	. .	1·7	2·0
1936	. .	2·2	2·4
1937	. .	3·0	2·8
1938	. .	4·2	3·4
1939	. .	5·6	3·7
1940	. .	7·0	4·0
1950	estimated	21·1	5·2
1951	estimated	—	—
1952	estimated	17·0	3·7
1953	estimated	14·0 approximately	3·0
1954	estimated	14·0 approximately	2·7

The downward trend of these figures in the period 1950–54 was probably due to a streamlining of the economic functions of the police apparatus rather than to any significant cut in the apparatus itself. In view of the indirect evidence on which the post-war figures are based, they cannot be closely related to other evidence on the nature of the changes in police functions. It is not improbable, however, that there was a connection between the post-1950 trend in Budget allocations and the abandonment by the MVD of responsibilities connected with hydro-electric construction (probably in March, 1953) with highway construction (September, 1953) and with the operations of *Dalstroi*, the Far East industrial trust (probably in the summer of 1953). At the same time the 1950–54 figures as a whole are far greater than the pre-war ones, when, as has been already shown, the scale of police activity was scarcely modest. It is also probable that some of the expenditure on the more secret activities of the police is either not shown in the Budget totals or is incorporated under headings other than those mentioned. The post-1954 changes in the structure of the police apparatus must be presumed to have brought about some further reduction in its budgetary allocation though the downward trend is likely now to have levelled off.

SOURCES

1. RSFSR Laws, 1917, 1:15.
2. RSFSR Laws, 1918, 75:813.
3. RSFSR Laws, 1919, 13:133.
4. RSFSR Laws, 1920, 79:371.
5. USSR Laws, 1931, 33:247.
6. USSR Laws, 1932, 84:518.
7. USSR Laws, 1934, 36:283.
8. RSFSR Laws, 1935, 41:349; USSR Laws, 1936, 36:318 (*a*) and (*b*).
9. Sorokin, pp. 255–6.
10. Sorokin, pp. 254–5, 258; *ESPZ*, p. 231.
11. *Vedomosti Verkhovnogo Soveta RSFSR*, 1965, No. 38.
12. Sorokin, p. 259.
13. Sorokin, p. 255; The subordination of the Militia to local Soviets is largely mythical. According to the RSFSR Procurator: 'Ten years ago the Militia was transformed into depart- of the Soviet Executive Committees. But many Executive Committees still take no interest in the Militia's activity. Thus the practice has developed whereby the Militia's work is directed and controlled only by the higher organs for the preservation of public order.' *Sotsialisti- cheskaya Zakonnost*, 1967, No. 5, p. 75.
14. *Pravda*, September 27, 1962.
15. *Vedomosti Verkhovnogo Soveta USSR*, 1962, No. 8.
16. *Partiinaya Zhizn*, 1965, No. 20, p. 16.
17. *Ibid.*
18. *Ibid.*, p. 18. Until 1956 there was a Political Department in the MVD's Chief Administration of Militia, with subordinate political depart-

ments in local Militia units. A Decree of June 5, 1956 (*Spravochnik Partiinogo Rabotnika*, p. 408), abolished this system and left responsibility for Party control of the Militia with local Party organs and Party organisations in the Militia. The pre-1956 system appears now to have been partially restored.
19. *Sovetskoye Gosudarstvo i Pravo*, 1965, No. 4, p. 70.
20. RSFSR Laws, 1922, 16:160.
21. USSR Laws, 1924, 12:105.
22. USSR Laws, 1934, 36:283.
23. *Gosudarstvenny Plan . . . na 1941 god*, Appendix No. 10, p. 90.
24. *Pravda*, May 28, 1965, in an article on Border Troops' Day, referred to 'sailor border troops', a 'border ship', and 'aviator border troops with modern planes and helicopters'.
25. *Vedomosti Verkhovnogo Soveta SSSR*, 1960, No. 34.
26. *Pravda*, April 27, 1966, announced awards to 'the Internal Troops, Internal and Convoy Guards of the RSFSR MOOP'.
27. RSFSR Laws, 1918, 80:842.
28. RSFSR Laws, 1924, 12:105.
29. USSR Laws, 1934, 36:283.
30. The Statutes on Military Tribunals refer, in Article 28, to the 'Convoy Guard of the MVD of the USSR'— *Pravda*, December 26, 1958. The continued existence of these troops is established, for example, by the awards in *Pravda*, April 27, 1966, to 'the Convoy Guards of the RSFSR MOOP'.

31. RSFSR Laws, 1922, 51:646; RSFSR Laws, 1923, 8:108.
32. RSFSR Laws, 1920, 79:371.
33. RSFSR Laws, 1924, 75:754.
34. USSR Laws, 1925, 77:579.
35. USSR Laws, 1930, 48:497.
36. USSR Laws, 1934, 48:372.
37. According to Sorokin, p.253, the MOOP are in charge of 'Internal Guards' as well as 'Internal Troops'.
38. RSFSR Laws, 1920, 79:371.
39. RSFSR Laws, 1922, 23:386.
40. RSFSR Laws, 1925, 68:539.
41. USSR Laws, 1931, 33:247.
42. e.g. reference to 'armed guards of enterprises' and to the 'armed guard of corrective labour camps and colonies and the warder staff of MVD prisons' by Chkhivadze, p. 166. *Vedomosti Verkhovnogo Soveta RSFSR*, 1966, No. 29, announced the award of a medal to a sergeant of 'the Internal Guard of the RSFSR MOOP', for 'self-sacrifice and bravery in the arrest of a particularly dangerous armed criminal'.
43. *Gudok*, December 11, 1966, has an article by a Deputy Head of the Administration of Military Guards of the Ministry of Transport.
44. Studenikin, Vlasov and Evtikhiev, pp. 286–7; Sorokin, p. 264; A Decree of December 24, 1966 (*Vedomosti Verkhovnogo Soveta RSFSR*, 1966, No. 52), awarded medals to members of the 'militarised Fire Guards of the Administration for the Preservation of Public Order of the Krasnoyarsk *Krai* Soviet'; A Decree of August 29, 1966 (*Vedomosti Verkhovnogo Soveta RSFSR*, 1966, No. 35), awarded medals to 'parachutist Fire Guards' of the Far Eastern Base for the Air Protection of Forests; Decree of March 3, 1962 (*Vedomosti Verkhovnogo Soveta RSFSR*, 1962, No. 9); Ugolovno-Protsessualny Kodeks RSFSR, Article 117.
45. *Pravda*, May 7, 1965.
46. *Sputnik Partiinogo Aktivista*, p. 42, refers to 'the special communications of the Ministry of Communications' used for the transmission of Party documents.
47. *Krasnaya Zvezda*, December 26, 1963, reported a Party conference of the 'Railway Troops of the Red Army'.
48. USSR Laws, 1931, 33:247.
49. USSR Laws, 1936: 316 (*a*) and (*b*).
50. *Voprosi Istorii KPSS*, 1963, No. 5, p. 82.
51. USSR Laws, 1936, 26:240 (*a*) and (*b*).
52. *BSE*, 2nd edn., Vol. 9, p. 308; *Komsomolskaya Pravda*, May 28, 1967.
53. USSR Laws, 1936, 36:316 (*a*) and (*b*) and USSR Laws 1936, 26: 240 (*a*) and (*b*).

III

Repression

An article by Lenin, in *The Workers' Newspaper* of December 31, 1910, bewailing the fate of a member of the Russian Social Democratic Party shot by Tsarist forces while smuggling weapons in Siberia for revolutionary purposes, declared:

'We are living under damnable conditions; when something such as this may happen; an important party worker, the pride of the party, a comrade who has given his whole life selflessly to the workers' cause disappears without trace and those nearest him, his wife and mother, his closest comrades, do not know what has happened to him for years; whether he is languishing somewhere in penal servitude, whether he has perished in some prison or other, or whether he has died a hero's death in a skirmish with the enemy.'[1]

The sufferings of the Bolshevik Party, and the country as a whole, under Stalin's purges far surpassed those they endured under the Tsarist régime. In these purges, the Soviet police forces were the main instrument, as well as occasionally the victims.

Soviet documentation on the specific contributions of the police forces during this period has been, not unnaturally, fragmentary. It was not until March, 1956, when Khrushchev made his secret speech to the Twentieth Party Congress that some part of the evidence was disclosed to a select Party audience.[2] Khrushchev confined himself to uncovering some—but not all—of the horrors of the period between 1934 and 1952; and Soviet historians, researchers and others, who took the speech as a signal for delving into other past misdeeds and misrepresentations, were swiftly called to order.[3] What has been told is, therefore, but a fraction of the whole.

Some twenty years after the events the Twentieth Party Congress was informed by Khrushchev that:

Ninety-eight of the 139 members and candidate members elected at the XVII Party Congress in 1934 were arrested and shot, and likewise 1,108 of the 1,966 delegates then present were arrested on counter-revolutionary charges;

[41]

In 1937–38, 383 advance lists of sentences to be pronounced, totalling many thousands of names, were submitted by Ezhov to Stalin;

Numerous Party leaders were tortured beyond endurance to induce them to confess to fabricated charges;

Many military commanders were 'annihilated' in 1937–41, including almost all those who had fought in Spain and the Far East;

The murder of Kirov in 1934, which served as the signal to unleash the terror, was a put-up job.

Trotskyism, which was the *leitmotiv* of the purge, had ceased to be a danger since 1927.

The actions denounced by Khrushchev constitute only one chapter, albeit the most lurid, in the history of Soviet police repression which began in 1917.

CHEKA OPERATIONS

From the creation of the Cheka in December, 1917, to its abolition in February, 1922, the Bolshevik State was either in the throes of civil war or dealing with its aftermath. The atrocities committed by the Reds had their counterpart in those committed by the Whites. But the sufferers were not only, or even principally, the opposing armed forces. On September 5, 1918, the introduction of the 'Red Terror' was announced. This was directed at the former nobility, the landowners, the bourgeoisie, and the clergy, as well as against the White Guards and opposition parties such as the Left Social Revolutionaries and the Mensheviks. The Cheka leaders, in any case, interpreted the Red Terror according to their own lights. A *Pravda* article of December, 1918,[4] by Latsis, a prominent Chekist, stated: 'Do not search for incriminating evidence as to whether a person opposed the Soviet with arms or with words. Your first duty is to ask him what class he belongs to, what were his origin, education and occupation. It is these questions that should decide the fate of the accused. This is the meaning and essence of the Red Terror.' Whatever the official attitude towards such an approach, the Cheka organs in practice enjoyed a great deal of autonomy and exhibited considerable disregard both for legal restrictions and for the general notion of 'revolutionary legality' as preached, for example, by the Sixth All-Russian Congress of Soviets at the end of 1918. As events showed, the Bolshevik Party leadership, Lenin included, made only ineffective and sporadic attempts to curb the Cheka, and neither the local Soviets nor the NKVD, nor least of all the

Revolutionary Tribunals, could act as a brake in practice, whatever they were supposed to do in theory.

No figure is available for the victims of the Red Terror, but it is thought they must have run into the tens of thousands. In fact the application of terror preceded the official announcement of it on September 5, 1918. Terroristic methods had been applied in Petrograd in December, 1917, before the establishment of the Cheka, when it was announced that 'attempts to break into wine cellars, warehouses, factories, stalls, shops, private apartments and so on and so forth will be broken up by machine-gun fire without warning'.[5] After the Cheka had been set up there were severe reprisals in the summer of 1918 after provincial risings in such places as Yaroslavl, Rybinsk, Murom, Nizhny-Novgorod and Penza. Only a few days after the assassination of Uritsky, head of the Petrograd Cheka, on August 30, 1918, the Petrograd papers announced that more than 500 hostages had been shot in Petrograd as a reprisal.[6] One of the Cheka leaders wrote in a pamphlet published in 1921 that during 1918 and the first seven months of 1919 Chekas in the provinces of Central Russia had executed 8,389 people.[7]

But there were other forms of coercion. One was the system of compulsory requisitioning of grain (or *prodrazverstka*) between May 9, 1918[8] and March 8, 1921.[9] As a 1950 Soviet textbook stated, this system was reinforced by the right 'to use armed force in the event of resistance to the surrender of grain and produce'.[10] Resistance was certainly encountered, and indeed in some regions the peasants staged mass insurrections (e.g. the Antonov rising, which was not finally suppressed until the summer of 1924).[11]

GPU AND OGPU OPERATIONS

From 1922 onwards the GPU and its successor, the OGPU, continued the task of 'liquidating the exploiting classes'—that is, members of the already dispossessed aristocracy and bourgeoisie, the priests, White Guard forces, and the Left-wing opposition parties. The elements of opposition within the Bolshevik Party were not yet generally engaging police attention, though the GPU in September, 1923, had already arrested certain Party conspirators.[12] The first of the political trials, that of the Social Revolutionaries, had indeed taken place during the GPU period, in June, 1922, but the main distinction between the GPU and the Cheka was the co-ordination of the GPU's work with the Party Control Commission. Disloyalty to the Party and treason to the State were becoming one and the same thing now that the Bolshevik Party had acquired a political monopoly.

In 1923 the GPU took action against private traders who had been encouraged to resume business activities under Lenin's New Economic Policy (NEP). *Izvestiya* said on December 28, 1923, that the GPU had arrested 1,000 'socially dangerous' persons and this had caused 'dismay and perplexity among the "Nepmen" '.[13] With the gradual abandonment of NEP in the late 1920s persecution of the 'Nepmen' increased, many being arrested on charges of hoarding gold and other valuables. As a standard history of the Communist Party stated: 'In 1926 and 1927 the picture had changed altogether. The economic policy of the Party and of the Soviet Government, while giving the working class and the poor peasantry a real improvement in their position, was striking harder and harder against the "Nepman" and the *kulak*, against the bourgeois elements, causing increasing discontent among them.'[14]

Nor was police action confined to private traders or even to the 'exploiting classes'. In 1922 the Supreme Court of the RSFSR complained:

'Recent statistics for 1921 show that the major percentage of those convicted by revolutionary tribunals belonged to the peasants and workers and that a very small percentage of convicts belonged to the *bourgeoisie* (in a broader sense). This ratio refers to all kinds of punishment, including execution by shooting.'[15]

Statistics published by the RSFSR Supreme Court for 1923[16] indicate that of those shot by order of the courts, workers and peasants constituted 70·8 per cent (workers 23·6 per cent, peasants 47·2 per cent), intellectuals and employees 20·7 per cent and others, including the bourgeois element, 8·5 per cent.

The OGPU was called upon to arrest 'ringleaders' and 'instigators' among factory workers when, as not infrequently happened, and particularly in 1923, stoppages of work occurred because of the workers' discontent.[17] The trade unions were accused of political indifference, of tolerance towards 'lagging' tendencies, and of alienation from the Party. The OGPU thereupon staged a series of trials to prove that breakdowns in pro-

[44]

duction were due to sabotage by technicians and part of con-
spiracies supported by foreign governments and groups to over-
throw the Soviet régime. Among these trials were the Shakhty
trial of May to July, 1928,[18] the 'Industrial Party' trial of November to December, 1930,[19] the Menshevik *Soyuznoye Byuro*
(Joint Bureau) trial of March, 1931,[20] and the Metropolitan-
Vickers employees trial of April, 1933.[21] There was also the
OGPU inquiry of March, 1933, into alleged subversive activities by employees of the People's Commissariat of Agriculture
and State Farms, resulting in the imposition of 36 death sentences and of 44 sentences of from eight to 10 years' deprivation of freedom.[22] These were token repressions, however, by
comparison with the purges of the later 'thirties. Even so, a
1929 circular of the People's Commissariat of Justice of the
RSFSR establishes that on December 1, 1928, a year before
the collectivisation drive began and several years before the
mass purges, the number of people deprived of liberty by the
courts in the RSFSR alone was 113,555.[23] This figure would not
include those sentenced by the OGPU Special Conference, or
those on whom banishment, exile or forced labour had been
imposed as administrative measures; and it takes no account
of those sentenced to death.

MASS COLLECTIVISATION

The mass repression carried out by the OGPU and other organs
of State during the period of the First Five-Year Plan took its
heaviest toll in the countryside. The policy of restricting and
squeezing out the *kulak* (pursued up to the summer of 1929)
then gave way to a policy of mass collectivisation and finally
to the decision to liquidate the *kulaks* as a class adopted at the
XVI Party Congress of June to July, 1930. Since the *kulaks*
constituted, as Stalin had pointed out in November, 1928,[24]
5 per cent of the rural population, that is to say more than a
million peasant families, this was indeed mass repression. The
kulaks were not allowed to join the collective farms but were
evicted, banished and, in the event of resistance, shot. Moreover, resistance to forcible collectivisation was by no means
confined to the *kulaks*, or even the 'middle' peasants; in many
areas the entire peasant population took part. As a standard
Soviet Party history stated: 'Everywhere the excesses aroused
discontent among the middle peasants and in some places

among the poor peasant masses, thereby strengthening the position of the *kulaks* who were being liquidated. On the basis of this content, combined with the desperate resistance of the *kulaks* to the carrying out of collectivisation and to the liquidation of the *kulaks* as a class, there occurred mass actions against collectivisation in various districts of the USSR.'[25]

Non-Soviet accounts of the mass collectivisation of 1930 and of the famine of 1931–33 are numerous.[26] There is, however, little official documentation. The mass repressions associated with it apply mainly to the years 1930–33, though collectivisation continued to be imposed by less drastic methods up to the outbreak of war in 1941. One official Soviet document dated May 8, 1933, throws light on the association of the OGPU with collectivisation.[27] This was a decree signed by Stalin and Molotov, and addressed to, among other bodies, the organs of the OGPU. It draws attention to mass repressions in the countryside; to the practice of mass arrests by the OGPU on the principle 'arrest first, then investigate'. It says that mass arrests must cease, and mass deportations give way to the deportation of individual families. It gives specific authorisation for the further deportation of 12,000 households, and directs that the current total of 800,000 people deprived of freedom must be reduced to 400,000 within two months. It also makes it clear that the maximum figure of 400,000 applies only to prisons and not to labour camps or colonies. The figure of 800,000 effective for May, 1933, consequently excludes the following categories of victims:

(1) those shot;
(2) those deported to resettlement areas (mostly Siberia and Central Asia) without deprivation of freedom;
(3) those exiled from a given area;
(4) those detained in forced labour camps or colonies;
(5) those sentenced to forced labour at their place of employment.

Since the above categories far exceeded the total held in prisons, the victims of mass collectivisation must be calculated in millions. The entire rural population of the USSR in 1926, acording to the official census of that year, totalled 120·7 million.[28] The number of *kulaks* (including their families), on the basis of Stalin's statement of 1928, would have been of the order of six million and, as the May, 1933, order establishes,

[46]

the mass repressions affected 'not only the *kulaks*, but also individual farmers and a proportion of collective farmers'. Finally, to the victims of police repression should be added those who died as a result of the famines of 1931–33.

POLITICAL PURGES AND THE NKVD

On December 1, 1934, soon after the OGPU had been absorbed by the NKVD, Kirov was assassinated. This event touched off a wave of arrests, executions and deportations that lasted until the end of 1938. The political terror of the late 1930s was aimed at crushing all opposition, actual, potential or putative within the Party, the Government and the armed forces. Its most prominent landmarks were the series of political trials staged between 1936 and 1938. Among the death sentences officially announced were:

August, 1936 ('the trial of the sixteen'): 16 executions, including Zinoviev, Kamenev, Smirnov and Mrachkovsky.

January, 1937 ('the trial of the seventeen'): 13 executions including Pyatakov, Serebryakov, Muralov and Drobnis.

June, 1937: Eight executions of military leaders, including Tukhachevsky, Yakir, Uborevich and Kork.

July, 1937: Seven executions of Georgian leaders, including Mdivani and Toroshelidze.

August, 1937: Execution of seven Georgian minor officials.

October, 1937: Execution of eight Georgian senior officials.

November, 1937: Execution of 10 officials of Abkhaz Autonomous Republic.

December 20, 1937: Eight executions, including those of Yenukidze and Karakhan.

December 31, 1937: Execution of eight Armenian officials.

March, 1938 ('the trial of the twenty-one'): 18 executions, including those of Yagoda, Bukharin and Rykov.

These sentences constituted only a signpost to the mass executions, deportations and imprisonment that went on simultaneously and of which the Soviet central and local Press gave numerous indications. These affected all branches of the Party and State apparatus. It has been estimated that of the commanding personnel of the Red Army, Navy and Air Force more than 30,000 were victims of the purges, including eleven Deputy Commissars of Defence and 75 out of the 80 generals and admirals on the Council of War formed in 1934 to assist the Commissar of Defence.[29]

The NKVD acted as the main instrument throughout. It not only had sole responsibility for the investigation of counter-revolutionary crimes but, under the law on terrorist acts introduced on the day of Kirov's murder, it took over the functions of the judiciary in such matters.[30] Such cases were to be heard 'without the participation of the parties', i.e. either of the defence or of the prosecution; investigation had to be terminated within 10 days; appeals were not permitted and the death sentence was the final pronouncement. The NKVD was, therefore, judge, jury and executioner.

In 1938 the NKVD was also among the accused; its head, Yagoda, was executed, his successor Yezhov disappeared without trace, and many of its own investigating officials were executed or sentenced to forced labour.

PRE-WAR AND WARTIME DEPORTATIONS

From 1939 onwards the mass repressions organised by the NKVD and its successors took the form of deportation. These operations were for the most part conducted by units of the border troops, internal troops and operational troops, with the participation, where required, of local Militia and army units, and with the aid of 'local brigades for assisting the Militia'.

After Soviet troops had occupied the eastern half of Poland in 1939 by agreement with the Nazi Government, mass deportations of Poles to forced labour camps in Siberia were organised by the NKVD.[31] These were followed in June, 1941, by others on an even larger scale organised in Latvia, Lithuania and Estonia which had been annexed to the Soviet Union in the summer of 1940.[32] They were carried out by troops of the newly-created NKGB and by NKVD convoy troops. Those officially earmarked for deportation as counter-revolutionary elements ranged from politicians to Red Cross officials and Esperantists.[33]

In 1940 there had been only sporadic deportations, for the most part of prominent Baltic officials, but it is estimated that as a result of the operations of June, 1941, some 170,000 people were forcibly expelled from the Baltic States.

The technique of mass deportations was also applied by the

Soviet police during the war to certain small nations long
incorporated in the USSR. The nationalities concerned were:

(a) the Volga Germans (deported in the summer of 1941);
(b) the Karachai (deported in the winter of 1943);
(c) the Kalmyks (deported in December, 1943);
(d) the Chechen-Ingushi (deported in February, 1944);
(e) the Crimean Tatars (deported in June, 1944);
(f) the Balkars.

Of the above only the deportations of the Volga Germans,[34] the
Chechen-Ingushi[35] and the Crimean Tatars[36] were announced
—and that retrospectively. The grounds for deportation were
collaboration or intention to collaborate with the Nazis. These
charges were applied to each of the peoples and eye-witness
accounts establish that they were deported as a whole, men,
women and children, by NKVD and State Security troops.

The record has since been belatedly and partially put straight.
Of the Kalmyk, Chechen-Ingushi, and Balkar deportations
Khrushchev declared in 1956:

'Not only a Marxist-Leninist but also no man of common sense
can grasp how it is possible to make whole nations responsible for
inimical activity, including women, children, old people, Communists and Komsomols, to use mass repression against them and to
expose them to misery and suffering for the hostile acts of individual
persons or groups of persons'.

The three nationalities named by Khrushchev with the addition of the Karachai were rehabilitated and allowed to return
from exile to their previous territories by Supreme Soviet Decree in 1957.[37] In 1962, Serov and other officials of the former
NKVD and NKGB were deprived of the decorations awarded
to them in connection with the deportation of the Chechen-
Ingushi.[38] The Volga Germans were rehabilitated by a Decree
of August 29, 1964, published in December, 1964, and the
Crimean Tatars by Decrees of September 5, 1967.[39] But unlike
the other rehabilitated nationalities they were not assisted to
return to their former homes or offered any form of compensation. No official pardon or restitution has been extended to the
largest of the deported contingents—those from the Baltic
States, though these last-named have been largely freed as the
result of other general amnesties (see chapter on Penal and
Economic Functions).[40]

After the Nazi capitulation, the NKVD and NKGB were responsible for supervising repatriation operations in Germany and Austria. Hundreds of thousands of Soviet nationals, some of whom had fought on the Nazi side, and others who had been prisoners-of-war or deported to Germany as *Ostarbeiter*, passed through NKVD and NKGB screening camps and were, in their majority, sent to forced labour camps in the Soviet Union. Soviet police organs also had a direct interest in the activities of the Soviet repatriation commissions in Germany, Austria and France.

In the Baltic States Soviet police forces had to deal with armed resistance by partisan groups and with peasant resistance to the collectivisation drive, which was intensified in 1948. From refugee evidence it appears that some 400,000 Lithuanians were deported towards the end of 1948, about 150,000 Latvians between then and the beginning of 1949 and in May, 1949, alone 35,000 Estonians.

There have been no post-war purges on an All-Union scale such as those of the 1930s. On the one hand there have been individual police actions directed against such disparate targets as 'bourgeois-nationalists', Jews, sections of the Soviet intelligentsia, resistance movements in the western Ukraine, and speculators in Government property. On the other hand there was also, as Khrushchev indicated in his secret speech, a continued succession of vendettas deriving from conflicts among the Soviet leadership. Thus the Zhdanov-Malenkov rivalry terminated, after the former's death in August, 1948, in the bloodletting of the 'Leningrad case' to which Voznesensky, Rodionov and many other senior and middle-ranking Party officials fell victim;[41] the Doctors' Plot of January to March, 1953, which was largely an anti-Beriya and anti-Semitic fabrication, continued the story.[42] There was also, just before Stalin's death, every appearance of a major purge of the Party leadership in the making—indeed, Khrushchev in his secret speech referred to Stalin's 'plans to finish off the old members of the Politburo'.

THE POST-STALIN ERA

Explanations for the absence of any major purge of the pre-war kind are not to be sought in any quiescent attitude on the part of the post-1946 MVD and MGB. The police under Stalin were masters of the situation: police controls were such that no opposition could ever organise itself, and Stalin did not live long enough to indulge in another periodical blood-letting of any sizeable proportions.

After Stalin's death it became clear that the only organisation that could immediately threaten the structure of Party control built up by Stalin was the police forces, then combined in one Ministry, the MVD, under the supreme control of Beriya. The post-1953 series of trials and executions precipitated by the arrest of Beriya in June of that year largely struck at the police apparatus. Its main landmarks were:

December, 1953. Trial and execution of Beriya and five senior police officials—Dekanozov, Kobulov, Goglidze, Meshik and Vlodzimirsky—for conspiring to seize power, contact with foreign intelligence agencies and terrorist acts.[43]

July, 1954. Execution of Ryumin, Head of Special Investigation Department of the KGB, for extortion of false confessions by torture.[44]

December, 1954. Trial and execution of Abakumov, Minister of State Security, and three senior MGB officials—Leonov, Komarov and Likhachev—for the extortion of false confessions and the fabrication of the Leningrad Case. Two other defendants sentenced to 15 and 25 years' corrective labour respectively.[45]

September, 1955. Trial and execution of Georgian Ministers of Internal Affairs and State Security—Rapava and Rukhadze—and four other Georgian senior police officials for aiding Beriya in his anti-Soviet activity and persecuting high-ranking Party members. The two other co-defendants were sentenced to 25 and 15 years' imprisonment respectively.[46]

April, 1956. Trial and execution of Bagirov, First Secretary of the Communist Party of Azerbaidzhan, and three Azerbaidzhani senior police officials for aiding Beriya, extorting confessions by torture, and putting honest Party members and others to death.[47]

In the last few years, publicity has been given in the West to the use in the Soviet Union of a method of repression favoured by the former Tsarist régime—the disposal of unruly intellectuals by their incarceration in mental hospitals and institutions. Not surprisingly it is difficult to document such cases from official Soviet sources, and to establish the rôle played in them by the police. Soviet sources do, however, provide confirmation for the existence of police 'psychiatric prison hospitals' and 'special psychiatric hospitals'.[48]

Since April, 1956, there has been no further major 'political trial'. Yet even with the police apparatus now transformed into an accessory of 'Socialist legality', it remains an instrument of the Party, and more particularly of the Party leadership. The requisites of the Party have often conflicted in the past with the requisites of justice. They may do so again. Leadership conflicts may still precipitate the use of police action the scope of which is, *per se*, not readily kept within the bounds set for it.

SOURCES

1. Lenin, *Sochineniya*, Vol. 16, p. 331.
2. The one and only official Soviet acknowledgement to date of Khrushchev's having delivered a speech to a 'closed session' of the Congress was a three-line statement to this effect contained in the Stenographic Report of the XX Party Congress published in June, 1956. The Central Committee Decree of June 30, 1956, 'On the Overcoming of the Cult of Personality and its Consequences', set out some of the general themes of the speech in directive form but carried none of the illustrative matter given in it.
3. e.g. Decree of the Central Committee of the CPSU of March 9, 1957, first published in June, 1957, in the *Spravochnik Partiinogo Rabotnika* (pp. 381–2), which penalised the Editorial Board of the journal *Voprosy Istorii* for ideological distortions in it from March, 1956, onwards.
4. *Pravda*, December 25, 1918. Lenin criticised this article as 'rubbish', but he nevertheless described Latsis as 'one of the best, experienced Communists'. Lenin, Vol. 28, pp. 365–6.
5. *Izvestiya*, December 19, 1917.
6. *Ibid.*, September 3 and 4, 1918.
7. Latsis, *Dva Goda Borby na Vnutrennom Fronte*, p. 75.
8. RSFSR Laws, 1918, 35:468.
9. *KPSS v Rezolyutsiyakh*, Vol. 1, p. 563.
10. Studenikin, Vlasov and Evtikhiev, p. 36.
11. Popov, part 2, p. 158.
12. Carr, Vol. 4, pp. 292–5.
13. *Ibid.*, pp. 121–2.
14. Popov, part 2, p. 321.
15. *RSFSR Supreme Tribunal, Military Bench directives, March 2, 1922; Collection of Circular Letters of the Supreme Tribunal attached to the All-Russian Central Executive Committee for 1921 and 1922 and of the RSFSR Supreme Court for 1923*, edited by Stuchka, p. 6; quoted by Gsovski, Vol. 1, p. 183.
16. *The RSFSR Supreme Court in 1923, Report by President Stuchka*, 1924, p. 26 and chart at end; quoted by Gsovski, Vol. 1, p. 184.
17. Carr. pp. 94–5.
18. BSE, 1st edn., Vol. 62, pp. 14–19.

19. *Ibid.*, Vol. 47, pp. 238–9.

20. *Ibid.*, Vol. 88, p. 826.

21. *Wrecking Activities at Power Stations in the Soviet Union: Special Session of the Supreme Court of the USSR, April 12–19, 1933.*

22. *Izvestiya*, March 12, 1933.

23. Circular of the People's Commissariat of Justice of the RSFSR, dated January 14, 1929, reproduced in an English translation in *A Selection of Documents Relative to the Labour Legislation of the Union of Soviet Socialist Republics*, p. 138.

24. Stalin, *Works*, Vol. 11, p. 138.

25. Popov, part 2, p. 407.

26. *See*, for example, Beck and Godin, pp. 13–15, and Maynard, p. 287 *et seq.*

27. Fainsod, pp. 185–8.

28. Podyachikh, p. 12.

29. Wollenberg, pp. 232–64.

30. USSR Laws, 1934, 64:459.

31. *See* accounts by Cardwell (pp. 93–114) and in *The Dark Side of the Moon.*

32. *These Names Accuse*, Appendix 7, p. 55.

33. *Ibid.*, p. 26, quoting NKVD Order No. 001223.

34. Decree of the Presidium of the Supreme Soviet of the USSR, August 28, 1941; *Vedomosti Verkhovnogo Soveta SSSR*, 1941, No. 38.

35. Decree of the Presidium of the Supreme Soviet of the RSFSR, June 25, 1946; *Izvestiya*, June 26, 1946.

36. *Ibid.*

37. Decrees of the Presidium of the Supreme Soviet of the USSR of January 9, 1957, ratified February 11, 1957— *Pravda*, February 12, 1957.

38. A Decree of April 4, 1962 (*Vedomosti Verkhovnogo Soveta SSSR*, 1962, No. 14), repealed the award of decorations to NKVD and NKGB officials on March 8, 1944, for the successful fulfilment of government assignments in the protection of State security'.

39. *Vedomosti Verkhovnogo Soveta SSSR*, 1964, No. 52; *Pravda Vostoka*, September 9, 1967.

40. Some indication of the involvement of the KGB in the granting of amnesties in general, and of those in the Baltic States in particular, was given in the communiqués on this subject issued by the Latvian and Estonian KGBs in January, 1956— *Sovetskaya Latviya*, January 11, 1956, and *Sovetskaya Estoniya*, January 13, 1956.

41. The Leningrad Case also constituted one of the charges included in the indictment of Abakumov in December, 1954—*Pravda*, December 25, 1954.

42. Discovery of 'plot' announced in *Pravda*, January 13, 1953; its exposure as a fabrication announced in *Pravda*, April 4, 1953, and in *Pravda* leading article of April 6, 1953.

43. Beriya's arrest announced *ex post facto* in *Pravda*, July 10, 1953, and the trial (December 18–23) and execution of Beriya and his co-defendants in *Pravda*, December 24, 1953.

44. Ryumin's arrest announced in *Pravda*, April 5, 1953, and his trial and execution (July 2–7) in *Pravda*, July 23, 1954.
45. Trial (December 14–19) and execution of Abakumov and co-defendants in Leningrad announced in *Pravda*, December 24, 1954.
46. Their trial and execution in Tiflis in September, 1955, were announced in *Zarya Vostoka*, November 22, 1955.
47. The trial (April 12–26) and execution of Bagirov and his co-defendants in Baku announced in *Bakinski Rabochy*, May 27, 1956.
48. *Sotsialisticheskaya Zakonnost*, 1957, No. 8, p. 20, referred to 'psychiatric prison hospitals of the MVD', and to the practice of ordinary hospitals of unloading difficult patients on to MVD hospitals. *Sotsialisticheskaya Zakonnost*, 1958, No. 7, p. 94, referred to the 'drawing up of new statutes for the special psychiatric hospitals of the USSR MVD', and to 'the central judicial psychiatric expert commission' attached to these hospitals.

IV

The System of Police Controls

The Soviet police apparatus has gained notoriety abroad from its association with the suppression of counter-revolutionary activities; a less spectacular, less draconian but more fundamental aspect of its activities is the maintenance and enforcement of the system of quasi-political controls on which Communist dictatorship depends for its existence. These controls concern the everyday life of every citizen; the main ones are the passport system, the frontier régime, the licensing system, and the police ancillary and informer networks.

THE PASSPORT SYSTEM

Under the law of December 27, 1932, an internal passport system was set up to be administered by the Chief Administration of Militia of the OGPU.[1] It is at present enforced by the MOOP Militia. Under the 'Regulation Concerning Passports' approved by the USSR Council of Ministers on October 21, 1953, 'all citizens over 16 permanently living in towns, workers' settlements, *raion* centres, inhabited points where the passport system is in force, and in all inhabited points of the forbidden frontier zones and frontier strips', are obliged to possess internal passports issued by the Militia.[2] The passport system is also in force throughout the three Baltic Republics and the Moscow *oblast*, and in 'many *raions*' of the Leningrad *oblast*.[3]

Entries are made in the internal passport showing the holder's 'social position', details of his military service, children under 16, marriage, divorce, places and dates of employment and of dismissals, and places of residence registered with the Militia.

Passports are of four types: permanent, for persons over 40; of 10 years' validity, for persons between 20 and 40; of five years' validity, for persons between 16 and 20; and of up to six months' validity, for those unable to provide proper documentation (e.g. birth certificates) necessary to receive a passport, and for those who have lost their passport. The renewal of one's passport once its validity has expired is 'a very long-drawn-out procedure', according to *Izvestiya*, which described how in one case it took eight days, three visits to the Militia and three visits to the 'house administrator' to achieve this.[4] There were suggestions after Khrushchev's fall that the passport regulations should 'long ago have been revised and simplified'.[5] But so far nothing has emerged.

For those who hold internal passports any change of domicile entails the registration of the passport with the Militia within 24 hours of their arrival. A registration fee is exacted. Similarly, absence from the normal place of domicile for any period exceeding one-and-a-half months, except for official business trips, leave, medical treatment, or to stay at one's *dacha*, involves 'de-registration' with the local Militia. De-registration is also obligatory for those sentenced to terms of imprisonment or deportation.

Those who do not possess internal passports, that is, in effect, collective farmers, are forbidden residence in areas where the passport system is enforced, save in the cases of those directed to work in urban areas, of Servicemen and of seasonal harvest workers. The only concession made to collective farmers is that they are allowed to stay in areas where the passport system is in force without a passport for a period not exceeding 30 days for such purposes as conferences, business trips or medical treatment, provided that they register such visits with the Militia and can show a certificate from their village Soviet stating their identity and the object of the visit. Otherwise, for any form of travel to a residence in an urban area, a passport has to be obtained from the Militia and this is of course contingent on official justification for such a move.

The local Militia may refuse to register a passport holder if he cannot provide the necessary documents showing he has already obtained living accommodation. These documents include: a 'house book', 'address lists', and a certificate from the 'house administrator' that accommodation has been made available. If registration is refused the passport holder must depart within three days or face criminal proceedings.

Possession of an internal passport does not of itself confer the right to visit or take up residence in any given area. Internal passports must be handed in by all those who are issued with foreign passports for travel abroad; by all those serving temporarily abroad (including, for example, the Aeroflot crews on international air routes, and the crews of Soviet merchant vessels); by persons entering hospital; by those called up for active military service; and by State Bank and Savings Bank officials who have charge of funds.

Among those obliged to collaborate with the Militia in running the passport system are: 'house administrators'; the commandants of houses and hostels, administrators of hotels, sanatoria, rest homes, hospitals, children's and invalids' homes; officials of village Soviets, and house owners. In Moscow, the caretakers of all residential buildings are obliged 'to inform the organs of the Militia about all cases of people who live without having registered and about all infringements of the city's passport regulations'.[6]

The 1932 decree establishing the system stated that among its aims was to relieve urban areas of people 'not engaged in socially useful labour' and 'of *kulak*, criminal and other anti-Bolshevik elements'. The present system is in fact more extensive than that of 1932. Far from having been relaxed in the post-1956 period, it has been tightened up. The head of the Soviet Militia stated in February, 1957, that the operation of the passport system by the Militia must be continued in full force.[7] In response to Khrushchev's own injunction of March, 1958, that movements of population needed to be more strictly controlled,[8] and in line with the introduction of laws to penalise idlers and speculators, the passport laws have been strengthened. Thus the new passport regulations for Moscow, passed in April, 1958,[9] directed MVD organs and the Moscow Soviet to 'discover and expel from Moscow those who avoid socially useful work'—this was particularly to be applied to those whose 'behaviour is unworthy' and 'who infringe the rules of the Socialist community'; moreover the corrective labour authorities were warned against allowing ex-inmates of camps and colonies to proceed to Moscow unless they had permanent residence and actual accommodation there before their arrest. Infringement of the passport system under Article 198 of the Penal Code entails sentences of up to one year's deprivation of freedom or corrective labour. Anything short of permanent registration in the area of domicile also virtually debars the applicant from permanent employment.[10]

The internal passport system restricts freedom of movement within the USSR, serves as an adjunct to the State direction of rural and urban labour, provides a brief case-history of the entire urban population, and can readily be turned against categories of the population deemed undesirable at any given moment.

The MOOP also control, with the Ministry of Foreign Affairs, the issuing of visas for foreign travel. Foreign passports are of three types: diplomatic, 'service', and 'general civilian'. The Militia is responsible for 'drawing up the documents for the exit abroad of Soviet citizens'.[11] Exit or entry 'without a proper passport or the permission of the appropriate organs' is punished under Article 20 of the 1958 Law on State Crimes entailing 'deprivation of freedom for from one to three years'.[12]

THE FRONTIER RÉGIME

The frontier areas established by Soviet legislation are extensive and police jurisdiction in them is paramount. Moreover, the KGB border guards and the local Militia have wide powers of repression.

The frontier system is regulated by the Statute on frontier guarding approved by the USSR Supreme Soviet on August 5, 1960.[13] It provides for a 'frontier zone' of unspecified extent in which special regulations apply, and entry into which is controlled by the Militia; and a 'frontier strip' running up to two kilometres back from the State border in which 'additional systems of restrictions' are enforced by border guards, and entry into which is controlled by border guards (Arts. 8, 10). The border guards also have responsibility for the 12-mile coastal frontier belt (Arts. 3, 29). They may 'erect special barriers, build roads, bridges . . . and other installations' (Art. 33). They have investigatory powers, and may carry out searches and confiscations, detain and cross-examine suspects and witnesses (Art. 32).

The border guards have the right to search and arrest even beyond the confines of the frontier strip and zones (Art. 31). All merchant ships within the 12-mile coastal limit are subject to inspection by vessels of the border guards if they fail to comply with special regulations for the coastal waters, and are liable to detention. Pursuit of ships refusing to halt when required is only broken off when entry into foreign waters is involved (Art. 36).

The border guards also have the right to use arms in the

event of armed attack and if other methods are insufficient to frustrate and detain illegal frontier-crossers, by land, sea or air (Art. 39).

Manuscripts and printed materials are also checked at the frontier control posts established by the border guards (Art. 11). In conjunction with the appropriate Ministries, the border guards issue regulations regarding customs control, medical, veterinary and plant control; and if there is danger of an epidemic may close sections of the frontier or establish a quarantine (Art. 23). The local authorities are obliged to provide the border guards with every assistance; and the local population, especially the People's Squads under the supervision of KGB and border guard representatives and the 'Young Friends of the Border Guards', organised by the Komsomol, provide active co-operation (Art. 40).

THE LICENSING SYSTEM

The police forces are charged with operating a complicated system of permits. These cover some activities which would properly fall within the competence of the police anywhere and others which cannot be said to do so. Among the former are the licensing of firearms, ammunition, explosives, poisons, and the supervision of public order; among the latter the licensing of printing establishments, supplies of printing machinery, engraving establishments, the manufacture of printing type and duplicating machines, all printed matter, plays and films and photography.[14]

Weapons and Explosives

Overall regulations of the production of, trade in and the issuing of weapons and explosives lies with the Militia under a law of December 12, 1924.[15] Thus shops supplying powder have to be licensed by the Militia;[16] the sale of smooth-bored[17] and small-calibre rifles[18] requires Militia permission; so do the manufacture and sale of daggers and broad-bladed knives.[19] The Militia control the opening and functioning of rifle-shooting galleries, firearm repair shops and firework shops.[20]

Poisons and Radioactive Substances

The manufacture, storage, issue and acquisition of strong poisons are dependent on the permission of the Militia under the relevant law of January 26, 1938.[21] More recently, radioactive substances have been included in the Militia licensing system.[22]

Printing Facilities

The Militia's powers are particularly comprehensive on the subject of printing processes.[23] Militia permission is required for:

(i) the opening of printing establishments;
(ii) the sale and the acquisition of printing, print assembling, and typing machines;
(iii) the opening of stamping and engraving establishments and establishments making seals and stamps;
(iv) the preparation by engraving and stamping establishments of seals with the Government crest; of seals for establishments or individuals; of seals for packages; of stamps for making entries in passports;[24]
(v) the sale, acquisition and use of duplicating apparatus.

Loss of official seals or stamps has to be reported to the Militia.

Since the relevant laws specifically direct that all printing and duplicating establishments must be in official hands, the exercise by the Militia of these powers reinforces the State monopoly of all publicity media.

CENSORSHIP

The earliest instance of police censorship was the compulsory despatch to the Cheka of three copies of each issue of all newspapers for censorship in 1918, failure to do so being punishable by closure of the paper.[25]

All printed matter, with the one major exception of Party publications (and even these had to be censored to safeguard State secrets) was made subject to censorship by the Chief Administration for the Affairs of the Poligraphic Industry, Publishing Houses and the Book Trade (abbreviated to *Glavlit*) in June, 1922.[26] The GPU in 1922,[27] and the OGPU in 1925,[28] were authorised to nominate, in conjunction with the Ministry of Education, two assistants to the head of *Glavlit*. OGPU's 'department of political control' was charged with 'fighting the distribution of works forbidden by *Glavlit*, underground publications, and the import of forbidden works from abroad'.[29] 'Preliminary' censorship[30] was exercised by *Glavlit*

[60]

plenipotentiaries in publishing houses, editorial offices, radio broadcasting organisations, telegraph agencies and a large number of other institutions, probably extending to libraries, universities and scientific institutes. 'Subsequent censorship' under a law of 1939 was the task of, among other authorities, the MVD.[31] The MVD also acquired responsibility under the law of 1922 for the 'confiscation of books banned in accordance with *Glavlit* lists'.[32] The relevant definition of books that came under this ban, drawn up in 1931,[32] extended to those which:

'(a) contain agitation and propaganda against the Soviet power and the dictatorship of the proletariat;
(b) disclose State secrets;
(c) arouse nationalistic and religious fanaticisms;
(d) have a pornographic character.'

Glavlit continues in being, as the 'Chief Administration for the Preservation of State Secrets in the Press attached to the USSR Council of Ministers'.[33] How far the KGB has inherited the censorship functions of its predecessors is uncertain, but it can be assumed that liaison continues between the political police and *Glavlit*, and a recent, well-informed refugee described in the British Press the KGB's interest in this field.[34]

Censorship of plays and films was effected by the Chief Committee for Repertoire (abbreviated to *Glavrepertkom*) which existed as a subsection of *Glavlit* from 1923 to 1934. An OGPU representative was included in the Committee and permanent seats (not further back than the fourth row) in all theatres and cinemas were to be put at the disposal of the 'political control department' of the OGPU and of *Glavrepertkom*.[35] All scripts and scenarios had to be shown to *Glavrepertkom* and the OGPU on demand. Film censorship apparently passed from *Glavrepertkom* to the Committee for the Affairs of Cinematography, set up in 1938,[36] and now known as the State Committee for Cinematography attached to the USSR Council of Ministers. In 1951, *Glavrepertkom* was abolished and its censorship of plays apparently passed to the Repertory-Editorial Department of the Chief Administration of Theatres under the USSR Ministry of Culture,[37] which was later succeeded by a similarly-named organisation.[38] It seems likely that responsibility for the censorship of plays and films lies with these bodies at the present moment, and that there is continuing activity of police organs in this direction.

[61]

Among the duties of the KGB is officially said to be: 'the taking of measures for the guarding of documents and of information constituting a State secret'.[39] It also 'works out regulations for the custody, use, transmission and destruction of various kinds of documents and material containing State and official secrets and controls the implementation of these regulations . . .'.[40] The MOOP controls 'the condition, custody and use of documentary materials kept in State and departmental archives'.[41]

Photographs

The Militia is responsible for enforcing the regulations drawn up in 1929 which forbid the taking of photographs in frontier areas, the photographing of aerodromes, naval ports, military dumps, military factories, defence installations, building complexes, tunnels, railway stations and any kind of construction on territory connected with the railways—unless special permission has previously been obtained.[42] The taking of photographs from the air is regulated by instructions issued by the Ministry of Defence; photographs can be taken inside official and public buildings only by permission of the appropriate administration. Local government authorities publish lists of special installations the photographing of which is forbidden.[43] The Militia has to enforce these regulations.

POLICE ANCILLARY NETWORKS

Important factors in the imposition of police controls are various ancillary police networks of agents, or auxiliaries openly recruited among the Soviet population.

The oldest of these networks is the system of 'rural executives' who assist the Militia in rural areas. Their functions were first systematised in 1924 and were further defined during the mass collectivisation period in an enactment of 1932.

Rural executives are appointed on a basis of one to every 300 inhabitants in all villages with a rural Soviet and on that of one executive for all other villages. They are nominated by local Soviets from local men of between 18 and 50 and women between 18 and 45—excluding those who have a court record, have undergone banishment or are under arrest—and serve for three months. Refusal to serve is a criminal offence. Their duties are to assist the rural Soviet and the Militia in fighting crime, in the protection of government property, in convoying people under arrest to their place of confinement, in supervising sanitary and fire precautions, and in carrying out local government and court orders. They are specifically obliged to inform the Militia of all 'crimes and occurrences' in the area. Their work is unpaid (though in the case of collective farmers they are credited for it in labour days) but they are released from all other duties for the period of their service.[44]

Brigades for Assisting the Militia

Voluntary Societies for Assisting the Militia and the Criminal Investigation were created in May, 1930, during the collectivisation drive and were attached to rural and urban Soviets.[45] In 1932 they were renamed Brigades for Assisting the Militia and put under the control of the Chief Administration of the Worker and Peasant Militia of the RSFSR.[46]

The brigades were supposedly voluntary bodies, membership of which was open to anyone 18 years old or over who had not been deprived of electoral rights, was not guilty of 'anti-social' actions, or had a court record. Such brigades were organised 'in factories, collective farms, State farms, educational establishments and other organisations and in individual inhabited localities on a production basis'.[47] Their tasks were described as 'assistance to the Militia in the fulfilment of its duties and active participation in the struggle against those who infringe the rules of the Socialist community, against instances of hooliganism and against other anti-Bolshevik occurrences'.[48] Their powers were probably wider. The 1930 Act stated that they were to take part in searches and roundups, and in convoying prisoners and ensuring order in public places. Moreover, they were empowered to take part in joint operations with the Militia. As one Soviet source stated, 'in the event of the utilisation of the brigades for assisting the Militia on operational work they can be issued with arms by the Militia, which arms are to be returned on completion of the work'.[49] The brigades also assisted the Militia in regulating traffic, in patrol work and in keeping order during official demonstrations and in providing the police with assistance at football matches, etc.

People's Squads

Under Khrushchev, greater efforts than ever before were made to involve the public in policing itself. The principal measure was the establishment by a Decree of March 2, 1959, of the People's Squads (*Druzhiny*) in place of the brigades for assisting the Militia.[50]

The Decree called for the establishment, 'on a strictly voluntary basis', in all enterprises, institutions, construction sites, farms, teaching establishments, transport systems and residential blocs, of 'people's squads for maintaining public order', composed of 'exemplary' workers, employees, collective farmers, students and pensioners. Control of the squads was entrusted to *raion* or town headquarters, consisting of representatives of Party and other organisations; and it was laid down that the squads and their headquarters should be headed 'as a rule' by local Party officials, and that they should work in contact with 'administrative organs' (i.e., the Militia). By 1964 over six million citizens had been enrolled in 150,000 squads throughout the country.[51]

Party control of the supposedly 'voluntary' squads is considerably more extensive than the Decree might suggest. The statutes of the squads for the RSFSR, adopted on March 30, 1960, declared bluntly: 'The organisation and control of the squads and their headquarters are carried out by Party organs.'[52] And according to a later pamphlet: 'In many cases the squads are headed by the secretaries of the Party organisations. ... At the biggest enterprises the squads are headed by the secretaries of the Party Committees. The *raion* and city squad headquarters, in the vast majority of cases, are headed by the secretaries of the respective Party Committee.'[53] Moreover, the personnel of all squad headquarters must be approved by the bureau of the respective Party Committee.[54]

It is not, perhaps, surprising that the squads encountered difficulties soon after their establishment: on the one hand the apathy[55] of many 'volunteers', and, on the other hand, the over-assertiveness of undesirable (careerist or even criminal[56]) elements who used the squads as a cover for their activities. The main fields of the squads' activity so far have been the patrolling of streets and public places, assisting the Militia in traffic and crowd control, and the campaign against drunks and hooligans.

Housing Administrations

The Militia works in close touch with 'house administrators' and with house caretakers and night watchmen.[57]

[64]

Administrative control over houses and flats is effected by the local Soviets through housing administrators appointed to exercise on-the-spot supervision. In the case of factory, university or trade school hostels the administrators are called commandants. In addition to their other responsibilities administrators are responsible for maintaining registers of all the inhabitants of their buildings and submitting 'address lists' to the Militia; for checking that all arrivals and departures are duly registered with the Militia; for being present during searches carried out on the premises by representatives of the KGB or the Militia; and for checking up on the identities of persons detained by the Militia. The administrators are liable to prosecution for failing to carry out these tasks.

The Moscow Passport System Decree of April, 1958, referred to connivance at infringements of passport regulations on the part of house administrators as the result of lack of control by the Militia and directed house administrators and commandants to exercise 'accurate execution of the obligations with which they are charged under the Passport Regulations' and to 'activise the work of responsible persons in the State who have the duty of supervising the observance by tenants of the rules of registration'; moreover, 'severe penalties are to be inflicted on house administration workers who permit contraventions of the passport régime, who check citizens out at the wrong time and incorrectly issue certificates, and, in case of abuse, to bring them before the criminal courts . . .'.

Police expulsions were officially credited with reducing the population of Moscow by 10,000 in the first half of 1958.[58] In March, 1959, the Moscow city Soviet was prompted to demand even stricter measures to limit the influx of outsiders with temporary residence permits, or no permits at all, and to prevent the unauthorised return of 'virgin landers'—i.e., citizens who had been induced, or directed, to leave the capital for the provinces.[59]

Caretakers and night watchmen are appointed and dismissed in urban areas by the house administrators by agreement with the Militia, to both of whom they are responsible.[60] Both caretakers and night watchmen are required to give all possible assistance to the Militia.

Among the duties of caretakers, established by the Statutes[61] on caretakers in RSFSR urban centres approved in conjunction with the Militia in January, 1959—in addition to such humdrum activities as snow-clearing and hanging out red flags on public holidays—are:

'(a) actively to help the organs of the Militia and the People's Squads in the preservation of public order;
(b) immediately to inform the Militia or People's Squads of all criminal activities or public misbehaviour known to them; to assist a Militiaman, in case of need, to escort arrested persons to the Militia office or People's Squad Headquarters; to keep places where crimes were committed in the state in which they were discovered until the arrival of Militia or Procuratura officials, etc.;
(c) to prevent people from living or spending the night in doorways, attics, and other non-residential places . . . and in the event of discovering such persons to inform the Militia;
(d) to check that no one in the building lives there without a passport or without registering, and to inform the housing administrator of any cases where this rule is broken;
(e) on the orders of the housing administrator to report immediately when summoned to do so by the Militia . . . and to participate in tours of the territory of the housing area carried out by the Militia.'

Street Committees

The Militia and the People's Squads can obtain assistance from the 'Street Committees' formed by local Soviets in both towns and villages and composed of representatives of the residents of a street or group of houses. The Statutes[62] for Street Committees in the Moscow *oblast*, adopted in 1960, obliged them 'to assist the organs of the Militia and People's Squads in the strengthening of public order and in observance of the passport system'.

The Komsomol and Other Auxiliaries

The Komsomol can usually be relied on to provide police auxiliaries. Apart from participating in the People's Squads and organising the 'Young Friends of the Frontier Guards', it has organised its own 'raids' and 'patrols'.[63] It provides one of the main sources of new recruits for the police organs themselves, which, since the Komsomol encourages delation and busy-bodying, customarily look to it for 'young talent'. An index list[64] of people and organisations decorated during 1966 'for excellent service in the preservation of public order' included several commanders and members of Komsomol 'operative detachments' and 'operative groups' who had, for example, 'shown bravery and courage in the preservation of public order and the fight against crime'. The list also included several 'voluntary collaborators of the Militia' and 'voluntary collaborators of the administration for the preservation of public order' (not members of the People's Squads) who had, for example, 'shown bravery and self-sacrifice in arresting an armed criminal'.

POLICE INFORMER NETWORKS

Parallel to the ancillary police networks the police forces maintain a system of secret informer networks. They are composed of 'secret collaborators' or 'unofficial collaborators' of the KGB, commonly known as *seksoti* (*sekretny sotrudnik*=secret collaborator). Khrushchev, in his 1956 speech to the closed session of the XX Congress, described a certain woman doctor Timashuk, who played a part in fabricating the notorious 'Doctors' Plot', as 'an unofficial collaborator of the organs of State security'. For obvious reasons, little is known from official sources about their methods of operation.

Police informers in some cases report direct to local KGB officers; in others they report to plain-clothes police agents. There is, however, one other important channel; the police points that exist within certain Soviet institutions. These points have in the past been variously referred to as 'special departments' or 'special sections', 'secret departments' or 'secret sections' in decrees establishing the structure of ministries and other official bodies; among such decrees are those relating to:

(a) Education departments of local Soviets;[65]
(b) Administration of Affairs of Art attached to the Council of People's Commissars of the RSFSR;[66]
(c) Ministry of the Local Fuel Industry of the RSFSR;[67]
(d) Ministry of the Timber Industry of the RSFSR;[68]
(e) Ministry of the Building Materials Industry of the RSFSR.[69]

These units have also been established in factories and other institutions as is confirmed by a reference in a 1946 Soviet textbook to 'the heads of secret departments or sections of factories, institutions and organisations'.[70] The heads of such units were responsible to the police, not to the manager or director of the establishment, and kept independent files on the personnel of the establishment.

The fact that no official post-1947 references to them are known to have appeared is no grounds for presuming that they do not continue to exist, though possibly in a different form and on a more reduced scale than used to be the case.[71]

Similar units function within the Soviet armed forces though official references to their existence are even fewer. In 1919 a 'Special Department' of the Cheka was given the task of 'combating counter-revolution and espionage' in the Army and Fleet, with subordinate special departments attached to military units and with its agents in foreign territory.[72] In 1923, there were 'special departments of military districts' attached to republican administrations of the OGPU.[73] Their subsequent existence was obliquely referred to in a 1953 legal textbook which mentioned the right of 'the organs of State security in the Army' to initiate legal proceedings against servicemen,[74] and, most recently, in a 1966 textbook[75] which described how representatives of the 'Special Department of the KGB' attended monthly conferences held by the Head of the Political Administration of certain Military Districts to hear reports on the state of discipline of the troops.

The KGB continues to maintain a watch over corrective labour colonies, according to unofficial reports, through its sections attached to the main labour colony complexes.

SOURCES

1. USSR Laws, 1932, 84:516, 517 and 518.
2. *ESPZ*, p. 309.
3. Sorokin, p. 259.
4. *Izvestiya*, November 28, 1964.
5. *Izvestiya*, January 15, 1965.
6. *Byulleten*, 1965, No. 15.
7. *Sovetskoye Gosudarstvo i Pravo*, 1957, No. 2, p. 39.
8. *Pravda*, March 15, 1958.
9. *Byulleten*, 1958, No. 11.
10. e.g. *Komsomolskaya Pravda*, August 28, 1959—article, 'Your Position Is . . . Uncertain.'
11. Sorokin, pp. 250, 258.
12. Law on Criminal Responsibility for State Crimes of December 25, 1958—*Pravda*, December 16, 1958.
13. *Vedomosti Verkhovnogo Soveta SSSR*, 1960, No. 34. An article in *Agitator*, No. 8, 1967, recently revealed an additional detail about the Soviet frontier régime—the existence of a 'ploughed and harrowed track-control strip [*kontrolno-sledovaya polosa*] (KSP) which runs along the Frontier'. A

ploughed strip runs along the frontier between the Soviet Republic of Moldavia and Rumania, according to *Sovetskaya Moldaviya* of May 27, 1967.

14. *ESPZ*, p. 396.
15. USSR Laws, 1924, 29:256.
16. Studenikin, Vlasov and Evtikhiev, p. 299.
17. USSR Laws, 1940, 31:777.
18. USSR Laws, 1938, 8:56.
19. USSR Laws, 1935, 18:141.
20. Sorokin, p. 257.
21. Decree of the Council of People's Commissars of the USSR, January 26, 1938, referred to in Vlasov and Evtikhiev, p. 231.
22. Sorokin, p. 257.
23. The two main laws are the decree of the Council of People's Commissars of the RSFSR, June 26, 1932; RSFSR Laws, 1932, 64:288; and the decree of the Council of People's Commissars of the USSR, July 21, 1935; USSR Laws, 1935, 40:341.
24. Referred to in *BSE*, 2nd edn., Vol. 32, p. 637; *ESPZ*, p. 317.
25. *Izvestiya*, March 3, 1918.
26. RSFSR Laws, 1922, 40:461.
27. *Ibid.*
28. RSFSR Laws, 1925, 71:561.
29. RSFSR Laws, 1923, 27:310.
30. RSFSR Laws, 1931, 31:273.
31. USSR Laws, 1939, 57:589.
32. RSFSR Laws, 1931, 31:273.
33. The abbreviation *Glavlit* has been retained though the full name of the organisation has changed, first to 'Chief Administration for the Preservation of State and Military Secrets in the Press' (*Slovar Sokrashchenii Russkogo Yazyka*, p. 126), and, more recently, to 'Chief Administration for the Preservation of State Secrets in the Press attached to the USSR Council of Ministers' (*Pravda*, December 23, 1966).
34. Leonid Vladimirov in the *Sunday Telegraph*, September 11, 1966.
35. RSFSR Laws, 1923, 27:310.
36. *Izvestiya*, March 24, 1938.
37. *Literaturnaya Gazeta*, October 15, 1953; *Ibid.*, March 3, 1955.
38. An official described as 'Chief Editor of the Repertory-Editorial Collegium of the Theatre Administration of the USSR Ministry of Culture' was referred to by *Sovetskaya Kultura*, July 11, 1964.
39. Sorokin, p. 245.
40. Sorokin, p. 252.
41. Sorokin, p. 254.
42. RSFSR Laws, 1929, 21:226.
43. RSFSR Laws, 1933, 45:187.
44. Vlasov and Evtikhiev, pp. 204–6; Studenikin, Vlasov and Evtikhiev, pp. 284–5; Sorokin, p. 283; RSFSR Laws, 1924, 28:266; 1931, 11:142; 1936, 7:40.
45. RSFSR Laws, 1930, 25:324.
46. RSFSR Laws, 1932, 38:173.
47. Studenikin, Vlasov and Evtikhiev, p. 285.
48. *Ibid.*
49. Vlasov and Evtikhiev, p. 207. For an instance of participation in operational work—*Sovetskaya Rossiya*, February 23, 1957.
50. *Pravda*, March 10, 1959.
51. *Partiinaya Zhizn*, 1964, No. 10, p. 11.

52. Dementev and Sergeev, p. 83.
53. *Ibid.*, p. 23.
54. *Ibid.*, p. 55.
55. *Sovetskoye Gosudarstvo i Pravo*, 1964, No. 6, p. 6.
56. *Komsomolskaya Pravda*, October 6, 1960, exposed a veritable campaign of terror waged by *druzhinniks* in Nikolaev. *Zarya Vostoka*, October 10, 1962, published references by Mzhavanadze, Georgian Party First Secretary, to criminals in the People's Squads.
57. Soviet laws on the duties of these functionaries are too numerous to list. A general description of their relationship to the Militia is given in Vlasov and Evtikhiev, pp. 207–9; and more recently in *Sbornik Zhilishchnogo Zakonodatelstva*, pp. 178–90.
58. *Byulleten*, 1958, No. 19, p. 18.
59. *Ibid.*, 1959, No. 7, pp. 5–6.

60. *Sbornik Zhilishchnogo Zakonodatelstva*, p. 185.
61. *Ibid.*, p. 186.
62. *Ibid.*, pp. 206–7.
63. *Izvestiya*, May 28, 1956, mentioned 300 'raids', in which a total of 100,000 people participated.
64. *Vedomosti Verkhovnogo Soveta RSFSR*, 1966, No. 52, pp. 1120–1.
65. RSFSR Laws, 1936, 14:97.
66. RSFSR Laws, 1940, 5:13.
67. RSFSR Laws, 1947, 12:38.
68. RSFSR Laws, 1947, 11:36.
69. RSFSR Laws, 1947, 5:14.
70. Vlasov and Evtikhiev, p. 231.
71. A 'Special Sector' of the Tadzhik Central Committee was listed in *Kommunist Tadzhikistana*, October 28, 1954.
72. RSFSR Laws, 1919, 6:58.
73. RSFSR Laws, 1924, 12:105.
74. Karev (D. S.), *Sovetsky Ugolovny Protsess*, p. 133.
75. *Prokurorsky Nadzor v SSSR*, p. 300.

V

The Police Apparatus
and the Judicial System

Since 1953 the Soviet police organs have been largely shorn
of extra-judicial powers dating back to the time of the pre-war
purges, and have lost the two special tribunals by means of
which they could entirely short-circuit the regular courts of
law. On the other hand the extent to which their participation
in regular judicial procedure has been circumscribed in the
post-Stalin period has not been as significant as had been
hoped by many Soviet lawyers; it still leaves them with considerable administrative jurisdiction over petty offences and
the KGB in particular with a broad and ill-defined competence
in the field of investigation.

EXTRA-JUDICIAL TRIBUNALS

The two tribunals associated with the police organs were the
Chief Administration of Military Tribunals of MVD Troops
and the Special Board.

The Chief Administration of Military Tribunals of MVD
Troops dealt not only with offences committed by police personnel, but also with a wide range of offences, including
offences against martial law, the evasion of mobilisation, the
disclosure of State secrets and the punishment of Red Army
deserters.[1] They were particularly active during the Second
World War, both at the front and in the rear areas and there
is documentary evidence of their involvement in the Soviet
punitive action in Latvia in 1941.[2] Their peacetime activities
must have been associated with districts where martial law
had been declared, or where large-scale punitive operations
were in progress. As was revealed in 1957, they were dissolved
by a still unpublished decree of the Presidium of the Supreme
Soviet of the USSR dated September 11, 1953.[3]

The Special Board was set up under the NKVD in 1934 and

was composed of the Deputy People's Commissar of Internal Affairs of the USSR, the plenipotentiary of the NKVD of the RSFSR, the Head of the Chief Administration of Worker and Peasant Militia and the People's Commissar of Internal Affairs of the Union Republic on whose territory the case arose. It was empowered to pass sentences where evidence was insufficient for the courts. The Prosecutor of the USSR or his deputy was to take part in its sessions and could protest against its decisions to the Central Executive Committee of the USSR, the decisions remaining meanwhile effective.[4]

The Special Board had the right to impose sentences of expulsion from the Soviet Union (in the case of foreigners), exile, and imprisonment in labour camps for, originally, up to five years. This limitation was later relaxed, but in any case labour camp inmates with Special Board sentences were seldom released. Trial and sentence were on the basis of written recommendations and provision was not made for the attendance of the accused.[5] In practice it dealt with the great majority of the millions of 'political' offenders, simply rubber-stamping the indictment. It could also lighten sentences on the recommendation of the appropriate NKVD organ.[6]

It continued to function after the war.[7] It was apparently transferred from the MVD to the MGB in March, 1952, and reincorporated into the MVD in 1953, when the two Ministries were merged. It was subsequently abolished in September, 1953,[8] though this was not officially revealed until 1956.[9]

The Special Board gave the police a means of imposing heavy sanctions where the offence was not officially indictable, the evidence was insufficient, or secrecy of proceedings was required. Its abolition means that 'treason trials' will have to be conducted within the system of regular courts.

EXTRA-JUDICIAL PROCEDURE

Equally, the police organs as the main instrument of political repression have also been divested of certain extra-judicial procedures of which they were previously able to avail themselves. The notorious law of December 1, 1934,[10] which launched the 1934–38 purge, and under which Beriya was tried in December, 1953, has been repealed as well as a lesser known law of September 14, 1937,[11] providing for a number of procedural limitations, including the presentation of the indictment one day before the trial, trial *in absentia*, with no possibility of appeal, in cases of wrecking, terrorism and subversion. All that now remains is that all espionage trials must still be heard by the Military Tribunals system supervised by the Military Collegium of the Supreme Court,[12] which can conduct proceedings *in camera*.

Police organs in the Soviet Union are responsible for carrying out searches, arrests and investigations before prosecution. Their influence makes itself particularly felt during investigations before trial.

In present Soviet legal theory investigation is divided into two stages: inquiry (*doznanie*) and preliminary investigation (*predvaritelnoe rassledovanie*). Inquiries alone may be sufficient for minor offences; the second stage of preliminary investigation is compulsory for the more serious crimes and for all crimes committed by juveniles. Among the organs authorised to conduct inquiries are: the Militia (which is responsible in the majority of cases); the MOOP (heads of MOOP corrective labour institutions may conduct inquiries in cases concerning the staff or inmates of such institutions, and the MOOP Fire Guards may do so in cases of fire or infringement of fire precautions); the Border Troops of the KGB (who may act in cases of infringement of the frontier regulations), and the KGB itself ('in cases assigned by law to its competence', as Article 117 of the RSFSR Criminal Procedural Code enigmatically puts it). Officials authorised to conduct preliminary investigations are: investigators of the MOOP (since April, 1963), of the Procuratura and of the KGB. Article 126 of the Criminal Procedural Code specifies which types of case are investigated by which kind of investigator, assigning to the KGB all 'particularly dangerous State crimes' apart from 'war propaganda', together with the more serious 'other State crimes' including, since 1961, economic crimes such as smuggling and illegal currency operations. The MOOP investigators deal with a wide variety of crimes, ranging from the misappropriation of State property to the spreading of venereal diseases, and were stated in 1964 to have been responsible for investigating 65 per cent of all criminal cases.[13]

Even though the police authorities are bound by the provisions of the Criminal Procedural Code and their investigations are subject to supervision by the Procuracy, they retain considerable latitude. Though normally required to obtain the prosecutor's sanction within 48 hours,[14] they can detain suspects for up to 10 days before preferring a charge.[15] In cases which attract sentence of deprivation of freedom they can detain the accused for up to two months before the case is brought to trial, and this period can be extended by a further period of from one to three months with permission from the appropriate level of the Prosecutor's Office or, in exceptional cases, it can be extended up to a total of nine months with the sanction of the Prosecutor-General of the USSR.[16]

Those undergoing investigation, whether or not a charge has been made, whether or not they are under detention, and whether the investigation is conducted by the police or by the prosecutor's representative, still have limited rights. The investigators, on the other hand, have considerable latitude. They take the decisions to initiate proceedings, to make an arrest, and to prolong the period of arrest—the Prosecutor's rôle is, in effect, that of giving or withholding sanction.[17] The information obtained during the investigation must not be divulged either to third parties or to the defence until the preliminary investigation has been completed.[18] Defence counsel is not admitted to the proceedings until the preliminary investigation has been declared terminated.[19]

Many of the above provisions introduced by the legal reform of 1958 are, however, an advance on their predecessors; also significant is the formal abandonment of the theory of the paramount importance as proof of the confession of the accused, which Vyshinsky had for so long successfully advocated.[20] At the same time incriminational leanings still persist,[21] defence counsel meet with obstruction from the police authorities,[22] and the dice are still somewhat weighted against the defence. Illegal arrests are by no means a thing of the past. In Minsk, the capital of Belorussia, for instance, according to the local Party newspaper, 'there are still cases of the illegal arrest of citizens and illicit searches'.[23] Quite recently a deputy Head of the Central Committee's Administrative Organs department admitted: 'instances of deliberately illegal actions such as abuse of authority, distortion of the truth in a legal case, falsification of material for the court or resulting from

[74]

investigations, and other shameful facts'.[24] Nor is it entirely the case that all political trials have ceased since 1956: in August, 1957, two defendants were tried and condemned to long prison sentences for offences committed in Latvia during the period 1899 to 1925 when there was no Soviet government in Latvia at all.[25] Trials of alleged war criminals still continue a quarter of a century after the events in which they are supposed to have been implicated.[26]

In addition, the Militia's wide administrative powers as regards the imposition of fines have recently been expanded.[27] Their administrative powers were also considerably increased by two decrees[28] of July 26, 1966, which make local Militia chiefs responsible for deciding within 24 hours of the arrest of a petty hooligan whether to impose a fine on him, or hand him over to a court, social organisation, workers' *kollektiv*, or comrades' court. Militia chiefs were also authorised to impose fines on persons appearing drunk in public. Moreover, 'systematic offenders against public order' could henceforth be summoned to the Militia 'for appropriate registration and official warnings about the impermissibility of anti-social conduct'. If necessary they could also be photographed and fingerprinted. Any abuse of the Militia's administrative powers is supposed to be checked by the Administrative Commissions attached to the local Soviets, but it frequently happens that these commissions are headed by the local Militia chief.[29]

SOURCES

1. Golunsky and Karev (D. S.), pp. 133–4, 136, 143, Vlasov and Evtikhiev, p. 259.
2. *These Names Accuse,* Appendix 7, p. 55.
3. *Partiinaya Zhizn,* 1957, No. 4, p. 68.
4. USSR Laws, 1935, 11:84.
5. *Ibid.*
6. *Ibid.*
7. Vlasov and Evtikhiev, p. 246.
8. H. J. Berman, 'Law Reform in the Soviet Union'; *The American Slavic and East European Review,* April, 1956.
9. *Sovetskoye Gosudarstvo i Pravo,* 1956, No. 1, p. 3.
10. *Pravda,* December 5, 1934.
11. *Vedomosti Verkhovnogo Soveta,* No. 9, 1956.
12. Article 9 (*d*) of the Regulations Concerning Military Tribunals dated November 25, 1958—*Pravda,* December 26, 1958.
13. *Sovetskoye Gosudarstvo i Pravo,* 1964, No. 6, p. 9.
14. RSFSR Criminal Procedural Code, Art. 122.
15. *Ibid.,* Art. 90.
16. *Ibid.,* Art. 97.

17. *Ibid.*, Arts. 97, 112, 116, 122, 127.
18. *Ibid.*, Art. 201.
19. *Ibid.*, Art. 47. Moreover the Soviet view of the rôle of defence counsel in court is an inhibiting factor:

    'The Soviet advocate must not be the accomplice of the accused in his desire to escape the consequences of his fully proved guilt . . . Not by justifying but by condemning the crime itself must a lawyer help in the education of man's moral qualities.' (*Moscow Radio*, talk, March 16, 1957.)

    'Frequently defence counsel assume the attitude in court of public prosecutors and virtually become second accusers.' (*Pravda Vostoka*, July 27, 1956.)
20. *Sovetskoye Gosudarstvo i Pravo*, 1956, No. 2, pp. 7–8.
21. e.g. Rakhunov, *Kommunist*, 1956, No. 7, pp. 48–9.
22. *Sovetskaya Yustitsiya*, 1958, No. 7, pp. 53–4.
23. *Sovetskaya Belorussiya*, October 28, 1964.
24. *Sovetskaya Yustitsiya*, 1966, No. 21.
25. *Sovetskaya Latviya*, August 4, 1957.
26. *Pravda* of December 15, 1966, announced the trial in Lvov of a group unmasked by 'Soviet Chekists', who 'became traitors' in 1941–2.
27. Under a Decree of March 3, 1962 (*Vedomosti Verkhovnogo Soveta RSFSR*, 1962, No. 9), the Militia may impose fines, without reference to the Administrative Commissions of local Soviets, for infringements of public order, of frontier regulations, road safety rules and the rules for the use of transport. In Moscow and the Moscow *oblast* they have authority to impose fines directly for infringement of the passport regulations (Sorokin, p. 262). Under a Decree of July 23, 1966 (*Vedomosti Verkhovnogo Sovet SSSR*, 1966, No. 30), they were given similar authority in respect of foreigners for infringing travel regulations.
28. *Pravda*, June 28, 1966; *Sovetskaya Yustitsiya*, 1966, No. 16, p. 26.
29. Barsukov, *Sovety Deputatov Trudyashchikhsya*, 1958, No. 3, p. 25; also 'The Fine Mania', *Izvestiya*, December 1, 1956.

VI

Penal and Economic
Functions of the Soviet Police

The first decree on the organisation of forced labour camps by
the Bolshevik régime was that of April 15, 1919,[1] although an
earlier decree (September, 1918) had directed that 'class enemies' should be isolated in 'concentration camps'.[2] The existence
of forced labour institutions in the Soviet Union has been
continuous ever since. After the Civil War when no legal limit
was laid down for periods of deprivation of freedom, the official
maximum term rose from five years in 1921 to 10 years in 1922
and finally to 25 years in 1937. It has now been reduced to 15
years.

There have been certain terminological changes; the terms
'forced labour', 'forced labour camps', and 'concentration
camps' were frequently used in legislation in the 1920s, but in
1933, by legislative enactment, the term 'corrective labour' was
substituted for 'forced labour'.[3]

DEVELOPMENT OF FORCED LABOUR INSTITUTIONS

The 1919 decree stated that persons sentenced by the Cheka,
the departments of management of the local Soviets of Workers'
and Peasants' Deputies, and judicial institutions should be im-
prisoned in 'corrective labour camps'. At this time it appears
that there were two separately administered systems of camps,
those controlled by the NKVD of the RSFSR and those under
the People's Commissariat of Justice of the RSFSR. The May,
1922, decree on the NKVD indicated the existence among its
subordinate organs of a 'Chief Administration of Forced
Labour'.[4]

In 1922 and 1923 the GPU was given powers of administrative banishment and exile for periods of up to three years.[5]
Exile involved either expulsion from a given locality, with a
ban on living in other specified places in the USSR, or expulsion

from the territory of the RSFSR. Banishment involved expulsion from a specified place to a specified place.

When in 1924 the first Soviet *Corrective Labour Codex*, that of the RSFSR,[6] was published there were still two separate forced labour systems; that of the Chief Administration of Places of Confinement (abbreviated to GUMZ) of the NKVD of the RSFSR; and that of the Chief Administration of Corrective Labour Camps (abbreviated to GULAG) of the OGPU (these were distinct from the OGPU's 'concentration camps' originally set up in 1919 in order to 'isolate' representatives of the Left and Right Social Revolutionaries, Mensheviks and Anarchists and of which the Solovetsky camps were the most notorious example).[7] The OGPU 'corrective labour' camps, as set out in the law of April 7, 1930, were for persons sentenced to over three years or persons 'condemned by a special decision of the OGPU'.[8] The corrective labour colonies appeared by inference to be mainly for those serving sentences of less than three years. In 1933 the *Corrective Labour Codex* at present in force was drawn up.[9]

Finally, as a result of the decree of October 7, 1934, the NKVD of the USSR gained control of every form and facility of imprisonment, forced labour, banishment and exile, including the colonies and other places of detention formerly administered by the People's Commissariat of Justice of the Union Republics and those administered by the formerly independent NKVDs of the Union Republics.[10] All the forced labour institutions thenceforward were grouped together under GULAG, including the labour-training colonies for juveniles established later.

When the NKVD was renamed MVD in 1946 the control of GULAG passed automatically to the latter, and it continued under the MVD after 1949 when the MGB took over several MVD functions. Only for a brief spell from May, 1953, was GULAG removed from its subordination to the police organs and put under the Ministry of Justice of the USSR at a time when Beriya had effected a merger of the MVD and MGB. As reliable refugee reports indicate, however, this experiment failed. The Ministry of Justice lacked the technical knowledge and experience necessary for administering this vast complex of camps and colonies, and for discharging the commitments under which forced labour was supplied to industrial and constructional projects. The confusion arising from the administrative changeover, not least among the MVD guards and camp staff, was one of the elements which, together with the general uncertainty after the death of Stalin, enabled large-scale strikes, involving tens of thousands of prisoners, to break out in Vorkuta and Norilsk in the summer of 1953.[11]

In April, 1954, the MVD resumed control of GULAG, the MVD camp staff having remained in their posts during the temporary transfer and the first Soviet experiment in removing forced labour from police control ended. The forced labour system had, however, to undergo further overhauling. In 1954 there were further strikes of varying magnitude in Taishet (January), Kingir (May–June), Dzhezkazgan (June) and Vorkuta (July). The process of weeding out the camp population by amnesties that had begun in March, 1953, was continued and a series of camp reforms undertaken. Organisationally this was reflected in the replacement in October, 1956, of GULAG by a Chief Administration of Corrective Labour Colonies (GUITK) of the MVD and the consequential move to replace camps as the main forced labour institution.[12] At present the MOOP, successor of the MVD, remains in charge of all corrective labour establishments under its Chief Administration of Places of Detention (GUMZ).[13]

Supervisory Commissions over the activities of corrective labour establishments, attached to the Executive Committees of the local Soviets, were set up in the RSFSR in May, 1957, and the other Republics followed suit.[14] It is claimed that these commissions, composed of representatives from the Soviets, trade unions and *Komsomols*, prevent any abuse of the system. But the commissions' recommendations are not mandatory and, as well as recommending remissions of sentence, they can also petition for the 'isolation' of offenders[15] or their transfer to prison.[16]

It was stated in December, 1958 (notably by Polyansky), that the time had come for new All-Union regulations on corrective labour and new Republican Corrective Labour Codices; and Rudenko, the Prosecutor-General, announced that new 'Statutes for the corrective labour colonies and prisons of the USSR MVD' had already been adopted by the Council of Ministers and entered into force. These USSR Statutes, however, were apparently never published; and it was not until nearly three years later that a very compressed summary was published of the Statutes which had been adopted for the RSFSR by a

Decree of August 29, 1961.[17] As for the All-Union regulations and Republican Codices, all that has emerged, eight years after the need for them was said to be urgent, have been occasional assurances that drafts have been or are being prepared.[18]

The RSFSR Statutes are said to have been framed with the object of increasing the severity of conditions for the hardened criminals who formed the majority of the colonies' inmates, and of providing possibilities for a more differentiated and effective approach to the re-education of various kinds of criminals.[19] The Statutes established four kinds of labour colony: with general, intensified, strict, or special régimes; and made the courts responsible for pronouncing which of these a criminal should serve his sentence in. There are also separate labour colonies for juveniles between the ages of 14 and 18: three types with varying degrees of severity, for boys; and one type for girls. Not only the courts but also MOOP have the task of selecting the appropriate type of colony for juvenile offenders. Criminals sentenced to prison are also divided into those undergoing a strict or a general régime.[20]

The differential treatment of criminals was further developed by the establishment in 1963 of 'colony settlements', to which model prisoners from all but the 'special régime' labour colonies can be transferred towards the end of their sentences.[21] As distinct from the colonies, the colony settlements have no militarised guard or cell-blocks. Inmates are able to wear their own clothes, receive visits from relatives and enjoy unrestricted use of parcel and letter services. They may have their families to live with them provided accommodation is available and may freely move about the settlement between reveille and lights-out.

The other side of the coin is that punishments for unruly elements in the colonies have been drastically stepped up. A Decree of May 18, 1961, laid down that actions disorganising the work of corrective labour institutions, i.e., terrorising fellow prisoners or attacking the administration, should be punished by eight to 15 years' imprisonment or by death.[22]

INMATES OF FORCED LABOUR INSTITUTIONS

The three principal milestones of Soviet forced labour legislation, the first Soviet *Corrective Labour Codex* of 1924, the law on Corrective Labour Camps of 1930 and the second *Correc-*

tive Labour Codex of 1933, clearly reveal the severity of the régime inside such establishments, the over-riding distinction between 'class-dangerous' and mere 'criminal' elements, and the further measures of punishment that could be imposed by the administrations of camps and colonies. These enactments, however, give no indication of the extent of forced labour or of the part it played in the economic operations of the NKVD/MVD.

Precise official Soviet figures relating to forced labour are few. Among those already referred to are the following:

1928, December. 113,555 persons undergoing deprivation of freedom by court sentence in the RSFSR.

1933, May. 800,000 people undergoing deprivation of freedom, *elsewhere* than in camps or colonies or in the form of banishment.

1933, August 4. 12,484 people 'freed from strenuous service of measures of social defence'; 59,516 had 'their terms shortened' by decree of the GPU in connection with the construction by forced labour of the White Sea–Baltic Canal.[23]

1937, July 14. 55,000 prisoners 'to be prematurely freed for having performed shock-work on the construction of the Moscow–Volga Canal' by decree of the Central Executive Committee and of the Council of People's Commissars of the USSR.[24]

Estimates of the total forced labour population in the Soviet Union vary but agree that the total must be reckoned in millions for the period of Stalin's rule. A highly conservative Western estimate, calculated solely from data given with the 1941 Soviet Plan of the National Economy (which omitted several major sectors), put the total for 1941 at three-and-a-half million.[25] A minimum of double that figure is a more usual estimate.

Since the war no official Soviet figures of any kind relating to forced labour have been available. The Baltic, Ukrainian and other wartime and post-war deportations, the purges of Soviet prisoners-of-war, of members of the Vlasovite army and of persons living in formerly German-occupied territory all contributed their quota to the forced labour population, which will certainly have run into millions.

Since 1953 there has, however, been a very considerable reduction in the forced labour population. The first large official post-war amnesty of March 28, 1953, decreed the release of those serving sentences of up to five years and of certain other categories of prisoners; this mainly affected those charged with ordinary crimes and to a lesser extent those sentenced for trifling political offences.[26] In April and July, 1954, two further decrees were passed;[27] the first permitted the release of persons undergoing sentence for crimes committed before they had reached the age of 18 after completion of one-third of their sentence, or reduction of sentence after completion of not less than six months of it; the second permitted the release on probation of persons on completion of two-thirds of their sentence. A subsequent amnesty of September 18, 1955, covered an important and numerous category of prisoners— namely, those serving sentences of up to 10 years on charges of wartime collaboration; this meant the large-scale rehabilitation of civilians who had remained in enemy-occupied territory.[28] There were further amnesties on September 20, 1956,[29] and November 1, 1957;[30] the former covering servicemen who had been sentenced on charges of surrendering to the enemy during the war; the latter providing for the release of a variety of offenders, including those serving sentences of up to three years, women with children of up to eight and expectant mothers, men over 60 and women over 55, and juveniles of up to 16.

The abolition of 'corrective labour camps' as such and the retention of colonies as the sole type of corrective labour establishment that was said to have taken place in October, 1956,[31] are unlikely to have been completed then and may have taken some time to carry out. There were references to sentences of detention in corrective labour camps as late as September, 1957.[32] It is known that camp clusters were in existence in early 1957 in the Archangel, Irkutsk, Kostroma and Molotov *oblasts* and the Komi and Mordvinian Autonomous Republics. But the terminological switch from 'camp' to 'colony' was made mandatory. On the one hand the new designation retrospectively sets the seal on the improvements in the 'camp' régime that had been effected largely in the period 1953–54. On the other the terms 'camp' and 'colony' had long since ceased to answer to the original demarcation of 1930 when the colonies were for those serving sentences of under three years; the latest Criminal Code provides for periods of detention of up to 15 years in corrective labour colonies. Particularly dangerous offenders are given prison sentences or may be transferred from colonies to prisons.[33]

It is certainly true that under the 1953–57 amnesties, as well as by virtue of other less-advertised, yet equally belated, measures of rehabilitation of the victims of Party purges, the forced labour and prison population has been considerably reduced. According to one senior Soviet official, in early 1957 it totalled 30 per cent of what it had been before the amnesty of March, 1953: of this total 50 per cent, it was said, were thieves, 20 per cent hooligans and the rest 'miscellaneous criminals'. Estimates for the pre-1953 period have always been in terms of several millions, account being taken of the immediate post-war increase. So on the basis of the above statement the total as late as 1957 seems likely to have been not less than one or two million.

There is certainly no question that the system of corrective labour is to be discontinued or even that its application is to be severely limited; the call is rather for its more rational enforcement. It can still be applied to offenders of 14 years and upwards,[34] though those under 18 cannot be sentenced to more than 10 years' corrective labour.[35]

The present extent and whereabouts of the colonies are not known—it is almost certainly the case that their numbers have substantially diminished in the post-1953 period. At the same time, in the post-1953 period there has been a lot of evidence showing that those then released ended up back in corrective labour institutions, in some cases because they were recidivists, in others because the fact of having a 'record' militated against their being able to settle down in steady employment. Equally the very stringent measures taken against those who offend against public order must also be partially offsetting the run-down in the corrective labour population. Finally the latest enactments have reduced the possibility of remissions of sentence: there had been complaints that such remissions had amounted to as much as three-quarters of the total sentence.[36] In 1958 it was laid down that the maximum remission should not exceed half of the sentence for offenders who had demonstrated their 'rehabilitation' and one-third for those convicted of especially dangerous anti-State crimes and other serious crimes, and that it should not be applicable to especially dangerous recidivists.[37] A Decree of May 5, 1961, excluded persons sentenced for especially dangerous anti-State crimes from any remission of their sentences at all.[38] Also now excluded were: persons sentenced for banditry; currency-forging; illegal foreign currency operations; large-scale theft of State property; the worst kinds of murder, rape and bribery; and robbery with violence. To this list were later (July, 1962) added persons sentenced for disorganising the work of corrective labour institutions, and for grave attacks on Militiamen or members of People's Squads.[39]

The slate has by no means been wiped clean. Quite apart from the incomplete rehabilitation of those involved in the pre-war purges, the rehabilitation of other categories of the population has not been complete. The Crimean Tatars and the Volga-Germans have not been permitted to return to their former homes; the Baltic nationals deported both before, during and after the war may not all have been amnestied (see chapter on Repression). Moreover, a large section of the various categories released under the amnesties and otherwise have in effect exchanged forced labour for forced settlement. Many were not repatriated but directed to reside in a specified area which they cannot leave without special permission—this applied to both the two major amnesties of March, 1953, and of September, 1955. Not only does this mean indefinite domicile in remote areas but all too frequently accommodation and living conditions which are only a degree better than those which they had left. Such resettlement areas included, as far as is known, the Aktyubinsk, Irkutsk, Karaganda, Magadan, Molotov, Stalinabad and Sverdlovsk *oblasts*, the Komi and Mordvinian Autonomous Republics, the Krasnoyarsk *krai* and other areas, particularly of Russia in Asia. The Criminal Code retains both exile and banishment among the main punishments—though five years is the maximum term now provided for.[40]

ECONOMIC ASPECTS OF FORCED LABOUR

Up to 1954 the MVD, apart from administering the forced labour system, was also responsible for the use of forced labour on major constructional projects, operated its own enterprises with forced labour and served as a labour pool for other economic enterprises independent of the MVD. Article 101 of the RSFSR Corrective Labour Codex defined four ways of exploiting forced labour:

'(*a*) for hire in State, co-operative and social enterprises and institutions, on the basis of contracts between the enterprises

[84]

and the institutions on the one hand and the corrective labour
institutions on the other;

(b) in enterprises specially organised for this purpose by the corrective labour institutions;

(c) on mass work organised by contract between the corrective
labour institutions and State and co-operative authorities.'

The 1930 law defining the functions and organisation of corrective labour camps stated that the camp commandant was
responsible for 'the employment of the labour of prisoners in
the most rational way on economic enterprises run on self-
supporting lines out of the camp's own resources'.[41]

Among the major constructional projects in which forced
labour controlled by the NKVD and subsequently the MVD
played a major part were those of the White Sea–Baltic Canal
(1931–33), the Moscow–Volga Canal (1932–37), the Baikal–
Amur railway (1934 onwards) and the Volga–Don Canal (1950–
1952). With these tasks went also the construction of numerous
hydro-electric stations, factories, branch railway lines and new
towns and settlements in isolated areas of the USSR, both
before the war and after.

These major undertakings by no means exhausted police
exploitation of forced labour. The NKVD and later the MVD
had large-scale economic undertakings of their own, of which
the 1941 Economic Plan gave detailed proof.[42] The share
of the NKVD in total industrial production for 1941 was 1·2
per cent. This excludes NKVD gold production for which no
data were given. NKVD industrial activities extended to:

Chromium ore mining .	40 per cent of total USSR production.
Coal mining . .	3 per cent of total USSR production.
Oil production . .	2·7 per cent of total RSFSR production.
Timber procurement .	12 per cent of USSR total.
Catching of fish . .	4 per cent of USSR total.
Cement production .	1·3 per cent of USSR total.

Other NKVD activities referred to in the 1941 Plan included
the production of furniture, ironware, cameras and photographic paper, road construction machinery, agricultural
machinery, metal presses, railway sleepers, knitwear, shoes
and the transport of timber.

Earlier Soviet legislation had given glimpses of the extent
of the NKVD's industrial operations: a 1929 instruction of the
People's Commissariat of Agriculture provided for the utilisation of forced labour 'of persons sentenced thereto without

[85]

detention under guard' on forestry work;[43] a 1938 decree directed that the NKVD should increase its production of furniture, knitwear, blankets, shoes, canvas and photographic paper;[44] a 1940 decree transferred three cotton-producing State farms from GULAG to the People's Commissariat of Agriculture;[45] and another of the same year directed the NKVD to market all timber products prepared by GULAG through the agency of the People's Commissariat of Forests, 'except for the timber products reserved by the NKVD and its chief administrations under the plan for supplying the national economy'.[46] Accounts of Soviet refugees and of returned foreign prisoners-of-war confirm that up to 1953 the industrial activities of the MVD closely resembled in nature and extent those of its predecessor.

In the period 1953–54 the MVD lost control of the camps to the Ministry of Justice and its economic functions passed to other governmental bodies; though it later recovered the former, it did not recover the latter. The principal move in that direction was the transfer from its control of Dalstroi, the administrative organ set up in the winter of 1931–32 under the OGPU to organise the intensive mining of gold in the North-eastern region of Siberia, centred round Kolyma and Magadan. Forced labour activities in this area had subsequently been extended to railway and road construction and the construction and operation of a whole number of industrial enterprises. Similarly, Dalstroi's jurisdiction had been extended to cover all North-east Siberia, excluding Kamchatka. The Dalstroi complex, as was evident from the 1941 Soviet Economic Plan, had been directly subordinate to the NKVD, independently of the GULAG chain of command. The MVD not only lost Dalstroi but was divested of the running of its other gold-mining concerns—up to 1952 it had been in total charge of this industry—and of its operation elsewhere in the Soviet Union of enterprises concerned with coal-mining, oil extraction and timber procurement. However, these moves must be taken to indicate the cessation of direct MVD control over industrial operations, and not the cessation of MVD control over local forced labour centres, nor necessarily over the hiring out of such labour to industrial enterprises on a contractual basis.

Though the MVD's Chief Administration for Hydrotechnical Construction, set up in 1940, was not overtly associated with any of the post-war hydro-electric construction projects, refugee accounts and internal evidence establish that the

MVD authorities participated in the construction of the Volga–Don Canal, completed in 1951.[47] It was believed that the *Gidroproekt* organisation[48] associated with the construction of the Stalingrad Hydro-Electric Power Station, begun in 1950, was an MVD body. In October, 1953, however, a reference to the MVD official (S. Ya. Zhuk) who was head of *Gidroproekt*, referred to that body as coming under the Ministry of Electric Power Stations and Electrical Industry.[49] Since this Ministry was created in March, 1953,[50] it may well be that the transfer of MVD responsibilities for hydro-electric construction to it, together, possibly, with the handing over of *Gidroproekt*, occurred around that time. Subsequently, as was indicated in April, 1954, the Ministry of Electric Power Stations and Electrical Industry was divided into two Ministries, those of Electric Power Stations and of Electric Industry.[51] Finally, the hydro-electric building enterprises and organisations subordinate to the Ministry of Electric Power Stations were transferred in November, 1954, to a new All-Union Ministry for the Construction of Electric Power Stations, which to all appearances replaced the MVD in charge of hydro-electric construction.[52]

SOURCES

1. RSFSR Laws, 1919, 12:124.
2. RSFSR Laws, 1918, 65:710.
3. *Ugolovny Kodeks RSFSR*, 1956, footnote to art. 20.
4. RSFSR Laws, 1922, 33:386.
5. RSFSR Laws, 1922, 51:646; RSFSR Laws, 1923, 8:108.
6. RSFSR Laws, 1924, 86:870.
7. RSFSR Laws, 1919, 12:130.
8. USSR Laws, 1930, 22:248.
9. RSFSR Laws, 1933, 48:208.
10. USSR Laws, 1934, 56:421.
11. *See* Scholmer and Gerland.
12. Statement by Kudryavtsev, Deputy Prosecutor-General of the USSR to Professor Berman—*The Daily Telegraph*, May 16, 1957. Also referred to in *Partiinaya Zhizn*, No. 4, 1957, p. 67.
13. Tikunov, pp. 66–7.
14. Tikunov, p. 129.
15. *Sovetskaya Yustitsiya*, 1958, No. 2, p. 55.
16. *Sotsialisticheskaya Zakonnost*, 1958, No. 4, p. 37; Article 8 (*m*) of the RSFSR Statutes on the Supervisory Commissions adopted in September, 1965 (*Vedomosti Verkhovnogo Soveta RSFSR*, 1965, No. 40). These Statutes gave the Commissions additional responsibilities, such as supervising the carrying out of exile, banishment and other forms of punishment not involving detention.
17. *Vedomosti Verkhovnogo Soveta RSFSR*, 1961, No. 37.

18. According to *Sotsialisticheskaya Zakonnost*, 1966, No. 9, p. 18, draft All-Union regulations are being prepared. According to Tikunov, p. 49, they have been prepared, and Republican Codices are being prepared.

19. Tikunov, pp. 16–17.

20. *Ibid.*, pp. 173–4.

21. Decree of June 26, 1963 (*Vedomosti Verkhovnogo Soveta RSFSR*, 1963, No. 26).

22. *Vedomosti Verkhovnogo Soveta SSSR*, 1961, No. 21.

23. USSR Laws, 1933, 50:294.

24. USSR Laws, 1937, 46:187.

25. *Journal of Political Economy*, Vol. 49, October, 1951 (article by Naum Jasny).

26. *Pravda*, March 28, 1953.

27. Decree of the Presidium of the Supreme Soviet of the USSR of April 24, 1954, and July 14, 1954—*Ugolovny Kodeks, RSFSR*, 1956, pp. 129–30.

28. Decree of the Presidium of the Supreme Soviet of September 17, 1955—*Izvestiya*, September 18, 1955.

29. Decree of the Presidium of the Supreme Soviet of the USSR of September 20, 1956—*Vedomosti Verkhovnogo Soveta SSSR*, 1956, No. 19.

30. Decree of the Presidium of the Supreme Soviet of November 1, 1957—*Pravda*, November 2, 1957.

31. *Partiinaya Zhizn*, 1957, No. 4, p. 67; *The Daily Telegraph*, May 16, 1957.

32. *Sovetskaya Rossiya*, September 27, 1957.

33. *Ugolovny Kodeks RSFSR*, art. 24.

34. Bases of Criminal Legislation of the USSR and the Union Republics of December 25, 1958, Art. 10—*Pravda*, December 26, 1958.

35. *Ibid.*, Art. 23.

36. Speech by Zarobyan at Supreme Soviet session of December, 1958—*Pravda*, December 27, 1958.

37. Bases of Criminal Legislation of the USSR and the Union Republics of December 25, 1958, Art. 44—*Pravda*, December 26, 1958.

38. *Vedomosti Verkhovnogo Soveta SSSR*, 1961, No. 19.

39. *Ugolovny Kodeks RSFSR*, art. 53.

40. *Ibid.*, arts. 25, 26.

41. USSR Laws, 1930, 22:248.

42. *Gosudarstvenny Plan . . . na 1941 god.*

43. Instruction of the People's Commissariat of Agriculture of the RSFSR, June 1, 1929, reproduced in an English translation in *A Selection of Documents Relative to the Labour Legislation of the Union of Soviet Socialist Republics*, p. 141.

44. USSR Laws, 1938, 33:202.

45. USSR Laws, 1940, 2:75.

46. USSR Laws, 1940, 2:78.

47. *Pravda*, September 20, 1952 (list of awards to those who participated in the construction of the Volga-Don Canal, among them various MVD officials, including Serov, Bogdanov, Obruchnikov and Zhuk); *Pravda*, September 13, 1952, for list of signatories to obituary of V. V. Chernyshev.

48. *Pravda*, August 31, 1950.
49. *Izvestiya*, October 10, 1953 (list of candidates for membership of the Academy of Sciences of the USSR).
50. *Pravda*, March 7, 1953.
51. *Izvestiya*, April 28, 1954 (communiqué of the Supreme Soviet of USSR, April 27, 1954).
52. *Ibid.*, November 23, 1954.

VII

Operations Abroad

Operations abroad are the most complex and least publicised of all the activities of the Soviet police.* Virtually all available information comes from Soviet police officials or agents who have fled abroad, foreign agents recruited abroad or persons against whom such operations have been directed.[1]

The main categories of Soviet police operations abroad, including operations against foreign nationals within the USSR, are:

(a) the collection of political and economic intelligence;
(b) the collection of information on the activities of Soviet *émigrés* and the penetration and disruption of Soviet *émigré* organisations;
(c) the collection of scientific and technical intelligence;
(d) the penetration of foreign Intelligence services;
(e) the surveillance of Soviet citizens serving in or visiting foreign countries;
(f) the surveillance of foreign nationals within the Soviet Union, in particular members of foreign missions;
(g) the dissemination abroad of false and misleading information;
(h) tactical reconnaissance and counter-espionage across the Soviet frontiers.

THE CENTRAL APPARATUS

There is no single unified Soviet apparatus for Intelligence and counter-espionage abroad. The Soviet police apparatus, the Soviet Armed Forces and the Soviet Communist Party each had and have their own separate organisations. Clandestine operations abroad, however, have by and large been dominated by the State Security branch of the police. This allocation of

* In this context it is the State Security branch of the Soviet police that is principally referred to.

responsibilities dates back at least to 1934 when a separate Department of State Security (GUGB) was first created within the NKVD. In 1941 this department was transformed into a People's Commissariat (NKGB) and so put on the same hierarchical level as the NKVD. In 1946, in line with all the other People's Commissariats, it became a Ministry (MGB). In March, 1953, the MGB was merged into the MVD, but a year later the State Security branch resumed independent existence as the present Committee of State Security (KGB). In principle the State Security apparatus is supposed to leave the collection of military Intelligence to the Chief Intelligence Administration (GRU) of the Ministry of Defence; in practice, there is some overlapping, particularly in the economic, political and scientific fields. For a short period between 1947 and 1951 there was an abortive attempt to co-ordinate the activities of the two bodies through a Committee of Information attached to the USSR Council of Ministers and presided over by senior representatives of the Ministry of Foreign Affairs. Owing to jealousy and mutual suspicion, however, the experiment failed and at present it is probable that direct liaison between the KGB and the GRU is maintained without intermediate co-ordination.

OPERATIONS ACROSS THE FRONTIER

With KGB border guard formations there are Intelligence sections responsible for the collection of topographical information for tactical purposes within foreign territory bordering on the Soviet Union to a depth of about 30 miles. They are also expected to penetrate the local population on both sides of the frontier so as to forestall illegal frontier crossings and to detect hostile troop concentrations. For these purposes they organise clandestine agent networks. The importance of the work naturally varies with the frontier in question.

OPERATIONS IN EAST EUROPE

In Eastern Germany, where Soviet forces are still stationed, the State Security branch responsible for the political reliability and security of the Soviet Army is inevitably represented. The same was true of Austria before Soviet troops left that country. Since the duties of the KGB include protection of the Army from penetration by hostile agents and from sabotage, it is free to extend its activities among the local population. A special field for the recruitment of clandestine agents in such areas is represented by returning prisoners-of-war and civilian internees, and by refugees. The targets pursued in Germany have ranged from the disruption of *émigré* activities to the removal of German scientists to the Soviet Union.[2] Though only slight evidence is available of the extent of such operations, a number of cases have come to light. Of these the best-known are the kidnapping of Dr. Walter Linse,[3] head of the West Berlin Free German Jurists' Association, on July 8, 1952; and of Alexander Trushnovich,[4] West Berlin representative of a Russian *émigré* anti-Soviet organisation, on April 13, 1954; the assassination mission of Khokhlov, a captain in the MVD, disclosed in March, 1954;[5] and the murder of two prominent Ukrainian *émigré* leaders—Rebet, in October, 1957, and Bendera, in October, 1959—by the KGB agent Stashinsky, who defected to the West in August, 1961, and was sentenced to eight years' hard labour by a Karlsruhe court in October, 1962.[6]

In the other East European countries, as has been disclosed by, among others, a former lieutenant-colonel in the Polish Ministry of State Security, Jozef Swiatlo,[7] the Soviet Union maintained advisers and staffs attached to the local State Security service. These advisers closely scrutinised the operational plans and projects of their counterparts so that Moscow could countermand or support them. The 'satellite' relationship of these countries with the Soviet Union is now largely a thing of the past, but co-operation between the KGB and other East European intelligence services no doubt continues (as, for example, with the arrest of Wynne in Budapest) though probably on a less detailed and day-to-day basis.

OPERATIONS IN THE WORLD AT LARGE

The main State Security Intelligence effort against foreign Powers is directed from Soviet embassies and missions abroad. Within the embassies there is a representative of State Security, assisted by subordinate officials and non-professional collaborators who hold normal diplomatic or specialist appointments as cover for their clandestine activities. According to Kaznacheev, two-thirds of the personnel of the Soviet Embassy in Rangoon, when he defected from it in June, 1959, were members of the Soviet Intelligence.[8] Penkovsky claimed that 60 per cent of

Soviet diplomats abroad belonged to either the GRU or the KGB.[9] The CPSU Central Committee's department for Foreign Cadres under Panyushkin is believed to co-ordinate the foreign postings of all Soviet personnel and to provide cover postings abroad for KGB and GRU officials.[10] As a rule an attempt is made to secure for intelligence officials posts which give them the greatest latitude for their undercover work. Appointments which necessitate wide contacts with foreigners are therefore most suitable and it has been found that posts involving consular and cultural duties, *Tass* representation, travel agency work and the promotion of commerce and trade are favourite choices. While the nominal embassy rank of any State Security official need not correspond to his Intelligence service rank, nevertheless the senior representative usually has diplomatic status, his rank depending on the extent of the State Security representation as a whole. His identity will be known to the ambassador, but those of his subordinates or the operations on which they are engaged will not necessarily be known to the ambassador. This appeared to be the case in Canada from Gouzenko's evidence. In the past, ambassadors have themselves acted as senior Intelligence representatives, as was revealed by Khokhlov of Panyushkin, Soviet Ambassador to the United States from 1947 to 1952, and by Rastvorov[11] of Roshchin, Ambassador to China from 1948 to 1952, but this is exceptional.

From refugees such as Walter Krivitski, from former Communists such as Elizabeth Bentley, Whittaker Chambers and Alexander Foote, from ex-Intelligence officers such as Wilhelm Flicke, and from confessions such as that of Richard Sorge, it is clear that the Soviet Intelligence Service also runs espionage networks which have little or no contact with the embassies. These often have direct communication with Moscow and fit into the pattern of civilian life in the countries concerned.

The main targets for State Security abroad in the offensive field are ministries of foreign affairs and other government offices, industrial and scientific and technical research establishments. *Emigrés* of Soviet nationality are a special target for the representative of the *émigré* department and there are a host of collaborators engaged on internal security who are directed by a specialist. Some of the latter are designated to meet and receive reports from agents among the crews of Soviet ships calling at ports in a particular country.

The dissemination of false and misleading information is achieved largely through sympathetic persons employed in, or in touch with, journalistic circles. By these means articles in the non-Communist Press sometimes give the Soviet point of view under a cloak of innocent respectability.

OPERATIONS AGAINST SOVIET NATIONALS ABROAD

Mention has already been made of operations against Soviet *émigré* organisations in Germany and Austria.

All Soviet nationals abroad, whether working for or against the Soviet Union, are a matter of concern to the State Security networks. Pre-war illustrations of this were the kidnapping of General Miller, head of the Military Union of Former Tsarist Officers, in Paris in 1937;[12] the murder in Switzerland in the same year of Ignace Reiss, a representative of the Soviet Intelligence who had resigned and broken with the Communist régime;[13] the murder in Belgium in 1938 of Agabekov, another member of the Soviet Intelligence who had broken with the régime eight years previously;[14] and pre-eminently the murder of Trotsky in Mexico in 1940.[15]

Since the war the Soviet citizen abroad has automatically come under surveillance. This extends not only to Soviet Embassy personnel, as the Gouzenko and Petrov cases showed, but also to foreign Soviet colonies, as in the case of Oksana Kasenkina,[16] a teacher in the Russian colony in New York. Surveillance applies equally to Soviet trade union, cultural or sports delegations visiting foreign countries, to Soviet participants in trade fairs, international scientific congresses or other gatherings. All such groups as a rule include one or more persons responsible for keeping watch over the movements, activities and contacts of the others. These persons are not necessarily Soviet police officials seconded for these duties, but can be part-time agents acting on orders.

Surveillance extends also to Soviet Army units abroad and to the crews of Soviet ships. Units of the Soviet counter-Intelligence service exist in all Army units down to regimental level (independent battalions rank as regiments for this purpose). Below regimental level there are no full-time counter-Intelligence officers but there are 'secret collaborators' who co-

[94]

operate with the regimental 'special departments' (*osobye otdely*). These departments do not take punitive action on the spot, but have power to initiate the recall to the Soviet Union of officers or men who have committed security offences. These may cover a large number of actions, from fraternising with girls to reading anti-Communist leaflets, from political indiscretion to listening to foreign broadcasts. Soldiers are under strict discipline as regards visits to local cinemas, dance halls, cafés or public houses; similarly, Soviet sailors visiting foreign countries are, as a general rule, restricted in their shore leave and, when allowed ashore, are required to stay in groups of three or more. Since the identity of all Intelligence agents is painstakingly concealed and the penalties for security in-fringements are severe, the insistence on group activities serves as a considerable deterrent, even where, as must be the case, many groups do not contain a counter-Intelligence agent.

OTHER ASPECTS OF OPERATIONS ABROAD

Other foreign operations conducted by the Soviet police which have never been fully authenticated and on which the evidence is tortuous have included the forging and circulation of large quantities of foreign currency in the 1930s; sabotage in foreign ports; and the instigation of strikes. It should also be added that Soviet police operations against other countries have an internal counterpart in the very painstaking system of surveil-lance, official and unofficial, maintained over the movements of foreign representatives within the USSR.[17] Before March, 1953, this task was handled by a special department of the MGB. Since 1954, with the re-emergence of a State Security organ independent of the MVD, it is likely to have reverted to KGB jurisdiction.

KGB operations against selected foreigners took on a par-ticularly brazen character towards the end of Khrushchev's rule. The two most notorious incidents were the attempt to frame Professor Barghoorn of Yale University by planting documents on him outside the Metropole Hotel in Moscow on October 30, 1963[18] (on the intervention of President Kennedy, Barghoorn was later released and expelled from the Soviet Union); and the mustard gas attack on Herr Schwirkmann, an official attached to the West German Embassy in Moscow (he had been sent there to detect listening devices) while he was visiting the monastery at Zagorsk, on September 6, 1964.[19]

There is also some evidence for the existence of a KGB department for the surveillance and penetration of the tourist traffic, and of businessmen, journalists and delegations from the West.[20] Among the aims of this department are thought to be: counter-espionage and the recruiting of potential KGB agents for operations abroad; the isolation of Soviet citizens from Western influences; and ensuring that visitors depart with a favourable impression of the USSR. Penalties on foreigners for disobeying travel regulations in the Soviet Union have recently been stiffened by a Decree of July 23, 1966, which provided for sentences of up to a year's deprivation of freedom or corrective labour, or the imposition of fines of up to 50 roubles.[21]

SOURCES

1. *See*, for example, Bentley; Chambers; Dewar, Flicke; Foote; Kasenkina; Krivitsky; Orlov; Tokaev; Weissberg; Willoughby; Kaznacheev; *Report of the Royal Commission on Espionage; Congressional Record*, 1949, Appendix, pp. A723–41.
2. *See* Tokaev.
3. *The Times*, July 9, 1952.
4. The *Daily Telegraph*, April 15, 1954.
5. *Ibid.*, April 24, 1954, reporting Press conference in Bonn held by United States High Commission in Germany, April 22, 1954.
6. *Die Welt*, October 5, 1962.
7. *Tenth Interim Report of Hearings before the Select Committee on Communist Aggression.*
8. Kaznacheev, p. 79.
9. *The Penkovsky Papers*, p. 73.
10. *Ibid.*, pp. 74–196. References to the department for foreign cadres are rare. But one of its officials was included among the recipients of a medal for helping to build a road in Afghanistan in *Vedomosti Verkhovnogo Soveta SSSR*, 1965, No. 45.
11. *New York Herald Tribune*, February 5, 7 and 8, 1954; *New York Times*, August 14, 1954.
12. Dewar, pp. 1–20; Orlov, pp. 233 and 235.
13. Dewar, pp. 32–43; Orlov, pp. 232–3 and 235.
14. Dewar, p. 39; Orlov, pp. 233–4.
15. Dewar, pp. 111–43.
16. Kasenkina.
17. The *Daily Telegraph*, December 6, 1954.
18. *The Times*, November 13 and 18, 1963.
19. *Die Welt*, October 14, 1964.
20. The *Sunday Telegraph*, August 8, 1965.
21. *Vedomosti Verkhovnogo Soveta SSSR*, 1966, No. 30.

BIBLIOGRAPHY

American Slavic and East European Review, periodical, New York.

Bakinsky Rabochy (Baku Worker), newspaper, organ of the Azerbaidzhan Party Central Committee, Supreme Soviet and Council of Ministers.

Beck, F., and Godin, W., *Russian Purge*, Hurst and Blackett, London, 1951.

Bentley, E., *Out of Bondage*, Rupert Hart-Davis, London, 1952.

Bolshaya Sovetskaya Entsiklopediya (Large Soviet Encyclopaedia), 1st edition, 65 volumes with supplementary volume on the USSR, Moscow, 1926–7; 2nd edition, 51 volumes, Moscow, 1949–58 (cited as *B.S.E.*).

Bomash, S., *Pravila Polzovaniya Zhiloy Ploshchadi v Domakh Gosudarstvennogo Zhilishchnogo Fonda i Obshchestvennykh Organizatsii* (Regulations on the Utilisation of Living Space in Buildings of the State Housing Fund and of Public Organisations), Leningrad Publishing House, 1953.

Bunyan, J., *Intervention, Civil War and Communism in Russia*, Johns Hopkins Press, Baltimore, 1936.

Byulleten Ispolnitelnogo Komiteta Moskovskogo Gorodskogo Soveta Deputatov Trudyashchikhsya (Bulletin of the Executive Committee of the Moscow City Soviet of Workers' Deputies), periodical, organ of the Executive Committee of the Moscow City Soviet (cited as *Byulleten*).

Cardwell, A. S., *Poland and Russia*, Sheed and Ward, New York, 1944.

Carr, E. H., *A History of Soviet Russia*, Vol. 4, *The Interregnum 1923–1924*, Macmillan and Co., London, 1954.

Chamberlin, W. H., *The Russian Revolution, 1917–21*, 2nd edition, Macmillan, New York, 1952, 2 volumes.

Chambers, Whittaker, *Witness*, Random House, U.S.A., 1952.

Chkhivadze, V. M., *Sovetskoye Voenno-Ugolovnoye Pravo* (Soviet Military Criminal Law), textbook for juridical higher educational establishments, Juridical Publishing House of the Ministry of Justice of the USSR, Moscow, 1948.

Congressional Record: The Sorge Spy Ring, extension of remarks of Hon. Harold O. Lovre of South Dakota in House of Representatives, Washington, February 9, 1949.

Dementev, N. V., and Sergeev, G. M., *Tebe Tovarishch Druzhinnik* (For You, Comrade Druzhinnik), Publishing House of the All-Union Central Council of Trade Unions, Moscow, 1961.

Dewar, Hugo, *Assassins at Large*, Wingate, London, 1952.

Die Welt, newspaper, Hamburg.

Dvadtsaty Syezd KPSS—Stenografichesky Otchet (Stenographic Report of the XX Congress of the CPSU), 2 volumes, State Publishing House of Political Literature, Moscow, 1957.

Entsiklopedichesky Slovar Pravovykh Znanii (Encyclopaedic Dictionary of Legal Knowledge), 'Soviet Encyclopaedia' Publishing House, Moscow, 1965 (cited as *ESPZ*).

Fainsod, M., *Smolensk Under Soviet Rule*, Macmillan, London, 1959.

Flicke, W., *Agenten funken nach Moskau*, Neptunverlag, 1952.

Foote, Alexander, *Handbook for Spies*, Museum Press, London, 1949.

Gerland, B., *Die Hölle ist ganz anders*, Steingrüben Verlag, Stuttgart, 1954.

Golunsky, S. A., and Karev, D. S., *Sudoustroistvo SSSR* (The Judicial System of the USSR), Juridical Publishing House of the Ministry of Justice of the USSR, Moscow, 1946.

Golyakov, I. T., (ed.), *Ugolovnoye Pravo* (Criminal Law), textbook for juridical schools, Juridical Publishing House of the People's Commissariat of Justice of the USSR, Moscow, 1943.

Gosudarstvenny Plan Razvitiya Narodnovo Khozyaikstva SSSR na 1941 god (prilozheniya k postanovleniyu SNK SSSR i Tsk VKP (b), No. 129 ot 17 Yanvarya 1941 g.) (State Plan for the Development of the National Economy of the USSR for 1941) (appendices to the decree of the Council of People's Commissars of the USSR and the Central Committee of the All-Union Communist Party [Bolsheviks], No. 129 of January 17, 1941); photostatic text published by the American Council of Learned Societies' Reprints, Russian Series, No. 30.

Gsovski, Vladimir, *Soviet Civil Law*, 2 volumes, University of Michigan Law School, 1948.

Gudok (The Whistle), newspaper, organ of the USSR Ministry of Railways and Central Committee of the Railway Workers' Trade Union.

Izvestiya (News), newspaper, organ of the Presidium of the Supreme Soviet (formerly Central Executive Committee) of the USSR.

Journal of Political Economy, periodical, published by University of Chicago Press.

Karev, D. S., *Sovetskoye Sudoustroistvo* (Soviet Judicial System), textbook for juridical higher educational establishments, State Publishing House of Juridical Literature, Moscow, 1951.

Karev, D. S., *Sovetsky Ugolovny Protsess* (Soviet Criminal Procedure), State Publishing House of Juridical Literature, Moscow, 1953.

Karev, M. P., and Fedkin, G. I., *Osnovy Sovetskogo Gosudarstva i Prava* (Bases of Soviet State and Law), textbook for engineering-economic institutes and faculties, State Publishing House of Juridical Literature, 2nd edition, Moscow, 1953.

Kasenkina, Oksana, *Leap to Freedom*, Hurst and Blackett, London, 1950.

Kaznacheev, A., *Inside a Soviet Embassy*, Lippincott, Philadelphia and New York, 1962.

Kommunist (Communist), periodical, organ of the Central Committee of the Communist Party of the Soviet Union.

Kommunist Tadzhikistana (Communist of Tadzhikistan), newspaper, organ of the Tadzhik Party Central Committee, Supreme Soviet and Council of Ministers.

Komsomolskaya Pravda (Young Communist Truth), newspaper, organ of the Central Committee of Ministers.

KPSS v Rezolyutsiyakh i Resheniyakh Syezdov, Konferentsiy i Plenumov TsK (The CPSU in Resolutions and Decisions of Congresses, Conferences and Plenums of the CC), 7th edition, 3 volumes, State Publishing House of Political Literature, Moscow, 1954.

Krasny Arkhiv (Red Archives), former bi-monthly, Central Archives of the USSR, Moscow-Leningrad.

Krasnaya Zvezda (Red Star), newspaper, organ of the Ministry of Defence of the USSR.

Krivitsky, W. G., *I Was Stalin's Agent*, Hamish Hamilton, London, 1939.

Latsis, M. Ya., *Chrezvychainiye Komissii po Borbe s Kontrrevolyutsiei* (Extraordinary Commissions for the Struggle against Counter-Revolution), Moscow, 1921.

Lenin, V. I., *Sochineniya* (Works) 4th edition, 35 volumes, Marx-Engels-Lenin Institute, Moscow, 1941–50.

Literaturnaya Gazeta (Literary Gazette), newspaper, organ of the Board of the Union of Soviet Writers of the USSR.

Maynard, J., *The Russian Peasant and Other Studies*, Gollancz, London, 1943.

Molodoy Kommunist (Young Communist), periodical, organ of the Central Committee of the Komsomol.

New York Herald Tribune, newspaper, New York.

New York Times, newspaper, New York.

Orlov, Alexander, *The Secret History of Stalin's Crimes*, Jarrold's, London, 1954.

Partiinaya Zhizn (Party Life), periodical, organ of the Central Committee of the Communist Party of the Soviet Union.

Podyachikh, P. G., *Vsesoyuznaya Perepis Naseleniya—1939* (All-Union Census of the Population—1939), State Statistical Publishing House, Moscow, 1953.

Popov, N., *Outline History of the Communist Party of the Soviet Union*, Co-operative Publishing Society of Foreign Workers in the USSR, Moscow-Leningrad, 1934.

Pravda (Truth), newspaper, organ of the Central Committee of the Communist Party of the Soviet Union.

Pravda Vostoka (Truth of the East), newspaper, organ of the Uzbek Party Central Committee, Supreme Soviet and Council of Ministers.

Prokurorsky Nadzor v SSSR (The Procurator's Supervision in the USSR), textbook for juridical faculties and institutes, Juridical Literature Publishing House, Moscow, 1966.

Report of the Royal Commission (Gouzenko Case), Ottawa, June 27, 1946.

Royal Commission on Espionage, Interim Report, Commonwealth of Australia, Sydney, October 21, 1954.

RSFSR Laws:

1917–38: *Sobranie Uzakoneniy i Rasporyazheniy Raboche-Krestyanskogo Pravitelstva Rossiyskoy Sovetskoy Federativnoy Sotsialisticheskoy Respubliki* (Collection of Statutes and Orders of the Worker-Peasant Government of the Russian Soviet Federative Socialist Republic), People's Commissariat of Justice of the RSFSR, Moscow.

1939–42: *Sobranie Postanovleniy i Rasporyazheniy Raboche-Krestyanskogo Pravitelstva RSFSR* (Collection of Decrees and Orders of the Worker-Peasant Government of the RSFSR), People's Commissariat of Justice of the RSFSR, Moscow.

1943–   : *Sobranie Postanovleniy i Rasporyazheniy Pravitelstva Rossiyskoy Sovetskoy Federativnoy Sotsialisticheskoy Respubliki* (Collection of Decrees and Orders of the Government of the Russian Soviet Federative Socialist Republic), People's Commissariat (Ministry from April, 1946) of Justice of the RSFSR, then (from March, 1947) Administration of Affairs of the Council of Ministers of the RSFSR, Moscow.

Sbornik Zhilishchnogo Zakonodatelstva (Collection of Legislation on Living Accommodation), Juridical Literature Publishing House, Moscow, 1963.

Scholmer, J., *Vorkuta*, Weidenfeld and Nicolson, London, 1954.

Selection of Documents Relative to the Labour Legislation of the Union of Soviet Socialist Republics, His Majesty's Stationery Office, London, 1931.

Slovar Sokrashchenii Russkogo Yazyka (Dictionary of Abbreviations of the Russian Language), State Publishing House of Foreign and National Dictionaries, Moscow, 1963.

Sorokin, V. D., *et al.*, *Sovetskoye Administrativnoye Pravo* (Soviet Administrative Law), Leningrad University Publishing House, Leningrad, 1966.

Sotsialisticheskaya Zakonnost (Socialist Legality), periodical, organ of the Prosecutor's Office of the USSR.

Sovetskaya Estoniya (Soviet Estonia), newspaper, organ of the Estonian Party Central Committee, Supreme Soviet and Council of Ministers.

Sovetskaya Kultura (Soviet Culture), newspaper, organ of the USSR Ministry of Culture and Central Committee of the Cultural Workers' Trade Union.

Sovetskaya Latviya (Soviet Latvia), newspaper, organ of the Latvian Party Central Committee, Supreme Soviet and Council of Ministers.

Sovetskaya Rossiya (Soviet Russia), newspaper, organ of the Central Committee of the CPSU.

Sovetskaya Yustitsiya (Soviet Justice), periodical, organ of the Supreme Court of the RSFSR, and the Juridical Commission attached to the RSFSR Council of Ministers.

Sovetskoye Gosudarstvo i Pravo (Soviet State and Law), periodical, organ of the Institute of State and Law of the USSR Academy of Sciences.

Sovetsky Flot (Soviet Fleet), former newspaper, organ of the Ministry of Defence of the USSR.

Sovety Deputatov Trudyashchikhsya (Soviets of Workers' Deputies), periodical.

Spravochnik Partiinogo Rabotnika (Party Worker's Handbook), State Publishing House of Political Literature, Moscow, 1957.

Sputnik Partiinogo Aktivista (Party Activist's Companion), Publishing House of the Ministry of Defence, Moscow, 1965.

Stalin, J. V., *Problems of Leninism*, Foreign Languages Publishing House, Moscow, 1953.

Stalin, J. V., *Works*, 13 volumes, Foreign Languages Publishing House, Moscow, 1952–55.

Studenikin, Se. S., Vlasov, V. A., and Evtikhiev, I. A., *Sovetskoye Administrativnoye Pravo* (Soviet Administrative Law), textbook for higher juridical establishments, State Publishing House of Juridical Literature, Moscow, 1950.

Sudebnaya Praktika Verkhovnogo Suda SSSR (Judicial Practice of the Supreme Court of the USSR), Juridical Publishing House of the Ministry of Justice of the USSR, Moscow, 1948.

Tarsis, V., *Ward 7*, Collins Harvill, London and Glasgow, 1965.

Tenth Interim Report of Hearings Before the Select Committee on Communist Aggression, House of Representatives, 83rd Congress, Second Session, United States Government Printing Office, Washington, 1954.

The *Daily Telegraph*, the *Sunday Telegraph*, newspapers, London.

The Dark Side of the Moon, Faber and Faber, London, 1946.

The Penkovsky Papers, Collins, London, 1965.

These Names Accuse, nominal list of Latvians deported to Soviet Russia in 1940–1941, published by the Latvian National Fund in the Scandinavian Countries, Stockholm, 1951.

Tikunov, V. S. (ed.), *Ispravitelno-Trudovoe Pravo* (Corrective Labour Law), textbook for juridical faculties and institutes, Juridical Literature Publishing House, Moscow, 1966.

Tokaev, G. A., *Stalin Means War*, Weidenfeld and Nicolson, London, 1951.

Trud (Labour), newspaper of the All-Union Central Council of Trade Unions.

Trybuna Ludu (People's Tribune), newspaper, organ of the Central Committee of the Polish United Workers' Party.

Ugolovny Kodeks RSFSR (Criminal Codex of the RSFSR), State Publishing House of Juridical Literature, Moscow, 1956, 1962.

Ugolovno-Protsessualny Kodeks RSFSR (RSFSR Criminal Procedural Codex), State Publishing House of Juridical Literature, Moscow, 1964.

USSR Laws:

1924–38: *Sobranie Zakonov i Rasporyazheniy Raboche-Krestyanskogo Pravitelstva Soyuza Sovetskikh Sotsialisticheskikh Respublik* (Collection of Laws and Orders of the Worker-Peasant Government of the Union of Soviet Socialist Republics), Administration of Affairs of the Council of People's Commissars of the USSR, Moscow.

1938– : *Sobranie Postanovleniy i Rasporyazheniy Pravitelstva Soyuza Sovetskikh Sotsialisticheskikh Respublik* (Collection of Decrees and Orders of the Government of the Union of Soviet Socialist Republics), Administration of Affairs of the Council of People's Commissars (Ministers from April, 1946) of the USSR, Moscow.

Vedomosti Verkhovnogo Soveta RSFSR (Gazette of the Supreme Soviet of the RSFSR), organ of the Supreme Soviet of the RSFSR.

Vedomosti Verkhovnogo Soveta SSSR (Gazette of the Supreme Soviet of the USSR), organ of the Supreme Soviet of the USSR.

Vlasov, V. A., and Evtikhiev, I. A., *Administrativnoye Pravo SSSR* (Administrative Law of the USSR), textbook for juridical institutes and faculties, Juridical Publishing House of the Ministry of Justice of the USSR, Moscow, 1946.

Voprosi Istorii KPSS (Questions of History of the CPSU), periodical, organ of the Institute of Marxism-Leninism.

Weissberg, Alex, *Conspiracy of Silence*, Hamish Hamilton, London, 1952.

Willoughby, Charles A., *Sorge—Soviet Master Spy*, William Kimber, London, 1952.

Wollenberg, E., *The Red Army*, Secker and Warburg, London, 1940.

Wrecking Activities at Power Stations in the Soviet Union: Special Session of the Supreme Court of the USSR, April 12–19, 1933, translation of the official verbatim report, State Law Publishing House, Moscow, 1933.

Zarya Vostoka (Dawn of the East), newspaper, organ of the Georgian Party Central Committee, Supreme Soviet and Council of Ministers.